Advance

How to Be an Artist . . .

"Do you dream of living a creative life but can't find the path to get there? Then buy this book! It's the absolute answer to your dreams."
—Arielle Eckstut and David Henry Sterry,
authors of *The Essential Guide to Getting Your Book Published:
How to Write It, Sell It, and Market It . . . Successfully*

"Whether your challenge is time, money, the distraction of social media, or, like Nagler, a multitude of talents that demand attention and artistic expression, this book will gently guide you back on track to the expression of your true purpose. . . . Nagler gives simple advice with charm and good humor. A great primer for anyone walking the creative path."
—Pat B. Allen, author of *Art Is a Way of Knowing*

"JoAnneh Nagler offers those longing to support their lives through their art the principles and practices for freeing their minds and wholeheartedly devoting their energies to delivering their gifts to the world."
—Michael Bernard Beckwith,
author of *Life Visioning* and *Spiritual Liberation*

"As a working artist for over 25 years, I have to admit that this book called my attention to some unproductive habits I have developed. It made me consider, 'What do I truly want in my life?' JoAnneh Nagler lovingly provides motivating guidance and practical methods to create or tune up a life-long, authentic, sustainable, and joyful artistic practice."
—Beth Grossman, visual and participatory performance artist

Dear Rich—

We walk the same path—as artists, discoverers, trail-blazers—and it is my incredible good luck (and my joy) to have found you there, and to have become your friend. Your spirit as a searching creator inspires me, but even more than that, it's simply your spirit: pure love, humor, delight and passion. I am blessed to know you.

Love,
JoAnneh

JOANNEH NAGLER

HOW TO BE AN
ARTIST
WITHOUT LOSING YOUR MIND, YOUR SHIRT, OR YOUR CREATIVE COMPASS

A Practical Guide

THE COUNTRYMAN PRESS

A division of W. W. Norton & Company

Independent Publishers Since 1923

*To Michael—for every endless gift of
love and artistry you give to me.*

For information about permission to reproduce
selections from this book, write to Permissions,
The Countryman Press, 500 Fifth Avenue, New York, NY 10110

For information about special discounts for bulk purchases,
please contact W. W. Norton Special Sales at
specialsales@wwnorton.com or 800-233-4830

Book design by Ellen Cipriano
Manufacturing by Berryville Graphics

Library of Congress Cataloging-in-Publication Data

Names: Nagler, JoAnneh, author.
Title: How to be an artist without losing your mind, your shirt, or your
creative compass : a practical guide / JoAnneh Nagler.
Description: Woodstock, VT : The Countryman
Press, 2016. | Includes index.
Identifiers: LCCN 2015040716 | ISBN 9781581573671 (pbk.)
Subjects: LCSH: Artists—Vocational guidance. | Artists—Psychology.
|Work-life balance.
Classification: LCC NX163 .N34 2016 | DDC 700.1—dc23
LC record available at http://lccn.loc.gov/2015040716

The Countryman Press
www.countrymanpress.com

A division of W. W. Norton & Company, Inc.
500 Fifth Avenue, New York, NY 10110
www.wwnorton.com

10 9 8 7 6 5 4 3 2 1

CONTENTS

INTRODUCTION   1

1: Answer the Call   7

It's Hard to Be an Artist.   9

It's About the Work.   10

When Your Artist Voice Is Calling, You're
    Supposed to Answer.   12

How on God's Green Earth Do I Answer "The Call"? 13

Living as an Artist Will Absolutely Test You.   15

Inspiration Is Not Enough.   16

You Can Learn to Become a Healthy Artist.   17

Nourish Your Artistic "Space."   19

2: Get a Day Job   21

Get a Day Job.   23

Be Willing to Be Good at More than One Thing.   24

A List to Live By.   25

The "Good People" Day Job.   26

The "Secondary Arts" Day Job.   29

Do Well, in Every Arena of Your Life.   30

Don't Bite the Hand that Feeds You.   32

Stop Complaining and Take Some Action.   33

Learn This Now: Slow, Steady Steps Are Better
     than All-or-Nothing Events.   35

3: Make Peace with Your Money   39

Money Clarity Buys You Time.   41

Anyone Can Add.   43

Don't Use Credit Cards to Fund Your Life.   44

Map Out What It Costs You to Live.   46

Cut Expenses to Buy Yourself Freedom.   49

Start Now.   52

Manage Your Money with Simple Tools.   54

Five Minutes a Day.   57

Use Whatever Works.   62

The Payoff.   65

Fund the Things You Love.   66

Live on Less for a Cause.   69

Know When to Say When.   71

4: Master Your Time — 77

Do Your Art, No Matter What Else Is Going on. — 79

All You Have to Do Is Listen and Act. — 82

Give Up the Privilege Myth. — 84

Do What's Important First, Not What's Urgent,
or "How the Hell Do I Get Started?" — 86

We've All Got 24 Hours, so Start Strategizing
Your Time. — 87

Get Practical and Get Real. — 88

Show Up for Your Art Hours as if It's a Job. — 92

We're in this for a Lifetime. — 93

5: Grow Some Work Ethics — 95

Don't Wait for Inspiration; Just Work. — 97

"Start Here": Get Some Tools to Help You. — 98

How Do You Know What to Work on First? — 101

Beat the Room. — 103

Support Your Artist's Work Ethic with a
Schedule and a Timer. — 105

When It All Goes to Hell. — 107

Show Up Until Showing Up Becomes Second Nature. — 108

Work without Regard for Outcomes. — 110

Practice Detachment. — 111

Know When to Set It on the Shelf.   112

There'll Be Days Like This.   114

Take a Break.   117

6: Map Your Art Life   119

Pin Your Points.   121

Map Your Art Life.   125

"I'm Just Not that Disciplined."   127

"No Pessimist Ever Discovered the
    Secret of the Stars . . ."   129

Know Your "Tells."   133

Allow for Enjoyment.   136

Get Time Clarity with an "Overall."   138

The Nuts and Bolts of Your Artist's "Time Map."   142

Working Your Map in the Real World.   148

What to Do if You Have a Crazy Schedule.   151

Learn What Works for You.   153

Set Boundaries.   155

Get Support.   159

A Last Look at Time Guidelines.   162

7: Motivate Yourself   167

When You Can't Stuff It Anymore. . . .   169

CONTENTS

Cultivate a Good Attitude.   170

Think Like an Inventor.   172

Do Your Art Because It's Worth Doing.   174

Separate Yourself from the Hobbyist.   176

Keep What You're Working on Close to Your Vest.   177

No One Gets to Judge You.   179

Acquire Wisdom.   181

Be a Moral Force for Your Art.   183

Practice Practical Inspiration.   185

Learn to Measure Wealth by the Freedom
    You Have to Do What You Love.   187

Make a Heaven on Earth.   189

INDEX   191

And what will you do with your one wild and precious life?

—MARY OLIVER

HOW TO BE AN

ARTIST

WITHOUT LOSING
YOUR MIND, YOUR
SHIRT, OR YOUR
CREATIVE COMPASS

INTRODUCTION

I never set out to be a creative person, I just *was* one. From the time I was seven years old, I knew I had something in me that was eating at me to create stuff—to draw, to paint, to sculpt, to design. I'd find myself in my family's yard in the dirt, making a paste out of mud and sculpting rudimentary objects, then coating them with a chalk I made from pink landscaping stones. I remember sitting at a picnic table at Girl Scouts, doing some charcoal sketching, and noticing, "Hmmm. I can do this."

Then I found I could sing; I could hear music. But my parents were also incredibly musical, so I thought everyone had musical talent.

As I grew up I found that I could write, paint, draw, cook, act, play the drums, compose songs, and in those days, it all came to me rather naturally. But I never thought of my artistry as a unique aptitude or as a special gift that I needed to share with my culture. I never thought to value it above my brain or to let it weigh in on the choice of how to spend my future.

Artists were poor, I was told. They struggled. They fought

with their family about whether they should pursue their art. They usually ended up giving it up—especially if they were women, to have kids; or, if they were men, to support a family. I thought the people who became artists had a trust fund or were born to parent-artists who supported them financially. I had no idea how to *become* one—a healthy one. All I knew was that I had talent and wanted to use it in some successful way, but I didn't have a clue in hell how to go about it.

My journals from the ages of 15 to 30 are chock-full of the quandary of what to do with the creative press of what came naturally. It was as if something inside me would not let me rest until I figured out how to do my art. I felt pregnant with it, distracted and even bullied by it, but I had no clue how to birth it.

There was no road map, no supports to help me *use* the gifts that wired me a little differently, and no guidance to help me find a path divergent from the usual workaday, buy-a-house, have-a-family, save-for-retirement road.

In college, every adult in my life was touting the same tagline: "Get a degree in *business*. That's what you're going to need." "Business is where the money is." And though wanting a piece of the postfeminist, businesswoman pie seemed the ticket to having an independent, self-assured life, business left me cold. Even when I succeeded at it—which I did, early and before college—I felt no love for it.

When I was 21, I had a voice teacher who took me aside and told me he thought I should pursue music full-time, as a lifelong career. But with no practical skills offered on how to follow that advice or how to live and support myself while I did it, I felt rootless and lost. I knew I was missing things I shouldn't be missing, but I couldn't practically put them together to build a livable life.

What was I supposed to do with the ubiquitous gifts of talent I was uncovering? How was I supposed to apply them? How could I make a living? With no one around to help me learn how to make the choices that mattered to me, how could I know whether I was making the right ones? And just how could I fend off poverty if I wanted to pursue my artistry and still live a decent life?

Years passed in which I missed the bold, brash road signs about my creative nature that were dumped into my path, years in which I was miserably trying to fit myself into professions that squeezed me into pretzel positions that truly made my soul ache.

By my mid-30s I had worked as a restaurant professional, a sales rep, a counselor, a nonprofit fundraiser, a grant writer, a personal chef, a fitness trainer, a classified ads editor, a clinic coordinator, and more. But I felt like a pretender: I could sell myself as a worker, but I had no long-term commitment to the work. I was tormented by the fear that I was wasting my life.

By then I had also worked intermittently ("on the side," as I thought of it then) as an actor, writer, and singer—all for very little money. But I had yet to step out; I had not yet learned to listen and take the steps needed to put solid supports under my feet to do my art consistently.

It would take me almost three decades to stop doing what I thought I was "supposed to do" and learn to use the creative skills I knew I had been given to live my life with art at the center. It meant I had to get real about having a day job I could live with. It meant I had to live more simply, on less money, to buy myself art time. It meant I had to stop trying to be everything to everyone else and start crafting my own path—one that had not been blazed before, one that had no dotted lines showing me how to beat back the underbrush.

It took every ounce of strength I had in both spirit and will to right my ship and turn my life back toward art.

For some years now, I have been living my life with artistry as my guiding principle. And every experience I have ever had—good and bad—gets added to the mix, enriches my creativity, and lifts my history into something I claim as good.

But when I look back at the winding track of my life—at the arduousness of it financially, emotionally, and spiritually—I wish I had had a guidepost, a teacher, a book, or a practice that could have helped me understand what it is to live as a creative person. Something to help me learn that I'm not alone, that there are tools that can be employed to live healthily with artistic gifts and desires, and that with steady steps I can achieve the joy of creative accomplishment. I wish—with all my heart—that I had not lost so much time resisting and searching.

I would have liked to have had a little guidebook I could keep referring back to for encouragement, guidance, inspiration, and direction: something to lead me out of the woods when I'm deep in and lost; something to give me practical tools to live by.

That's what I've crafted in this book: a set of simple principles to help us learn and remember what a gift it is to be endowed with creativity, what to do to keep our head in and heart uplifted, and what practical steps to take to manage our talent well. It's a book to help us put into place the steps and supports we need to make sure we don't lose our mind, our shirt, or our creative compass while we're on this road of artistry.

This book is for all of the creative souls who know what I knew—that they have artistic talent—and who need support to craft a life that lets them find, build, and grow their gifts.

The artist's road is about finding the path of love, not the path of duty; it's about honoring what we've been gifted with and building the courage to live the life we were meant to live.

The insights I have shared in this volume have changed my life and have brought me—finally, after a long road of insight-inspiring hardship—to artistic happiness. I hope they give as much to you as they have to me, and that they make your artist's road clearer and a whole lot easier to walk.

Remember this: It's never too late and we're never too old to have a happy ending—and our artistry is the brave, amazing, and visionary road that will lead us there.

1:

ANSWER THE CALL

It's Hard to Be an Artist.

Don't even fool yourself: It's hard to be an artist.

It takes all of our courage, all of our strength, and on many days, every last ounce of our physical and spiritual energy to make art.

Even when our ideas come quickly and abundantly, the materialization of the form may take hours, months, even years.

And many of us struggle with our ideas, too, as well as the physical out-picturing of the thing. We may see it, feel it, or even sense that something wants to birth itself out from inside us, but its amoeba-like, early-hours shape eludes us like a lover who stops by to wake up every passionate bone in our body and then forgets to call.

And once we really begin working on our art, the mountain we climbed to get started gets even steeper and harder to scale. Suddenly, it feels like we're climbing straight up into thinner and thinner air from absolutely nowhere. Our piece may need reworking 8, 10, even 12 times, or it may even need to be unraveled, scratched off, rewritten, painted over, pulled apart, or otherwise destroyed before the essence of the thing that really works makes itself known.

Then, there's our sense of composition: We're evolving, so our artistic vision is growing, too; it's changing all the time and can't be relied upon to stay the same any two days in a row. Since we're not relying on the intellectual, linear process of *A to B to C* to get this work out of our head and heart, it can be dizzyingly challenging to find a solid expression of the theme while the ground is moving beneath our feet and our vision is changing with it.

And let's not even get started with the how-to-live thing. Anyone who's ever tried to live as an artist knows the pitfalls. Money. Time. The pull of family obligations. Partners who don't understand our need to create and are angry at the time it takes away from a relationship or family life. Friends who look at us as if we've quite lost our mind to be putting so much time and effort into a venture with no particular promise of "success."

But there's a reason why we do our art, and a reason why the call is so strong. Our art is a call straight from the heart.

It's About the Work.

Take all of the romance we feel about art personally, add the cultural hype we heap upon ourselves, hoping our art will save us or propel us into stardom, then mix in a good dose of I-deserve-it prayers for instant success, and we will end up with a useless pile of you-know-what.

The truth about making art is infinitely more profound and much, much simpler than all of that hype and hope. Here it is: *It's about the work*. It's about showing up daily to engage in something that no one else can create, that has never been created before, and that no one—besides you—can deliver.

It's about acting on a vision.

And here's the sticky part. Since our voice and vision can only come from inside us—and that's where the good stuff lives—that means we're working on art that no one particularly wants yet.

And we must learn to work anyway, knowing that (1) there are no assured outcomes, (2) no one may ever give us credit or money for our efforts, and (3) there are no parameters and often no one to push us when we're inventing from inside the soul of our creativity.

What we learn—if we're lucky—is that we work because we *have to*, because it's necessary for our spirit, and because we are not happy people when we don't. Many of us have discovered the hard way that to bury the artistic call and shirk the work is to court desperation and misery.

Art matters.

In particular, it matters to us, its creators and its potential creators. It calls us from an unknown place, singing to us from a land of invisible melodies that only we can hear. It's special to be called as an artist.

Art—beyond the old adage that when the cities are burning, the people are running from them with their art in their hands—is precious. And it's precious not because of its monetary value, but because of its process. Because we sat down in fear and uncertainty and created something anyway. We had the gall and the courage to touch the hem of the divine by not only listening, but by *acting* on our God-given inspiration.

When Your Artist Voice Is Calling, You're Supposed to Answer.

Here's the thing about an artistic "calling": It's as if there's a voice from another dimension that's speaking to us—whispering at first, and if we're lucky, later on, torqueing up the volume in our inner ears—*insisting* that we get this vision out of the realm of the ethereal and into the real world.

If we're honest, many of us need to get pregnant with the call to act, to feel the press and harangue of the now not-quite-so-still-and-small voice that says, "For God's sake, you're dying to song-write so take some damn guitar lessons!"

Yet even with what seems like the resonance of a Greek chorus pounding away in our heads, chanting, "Take a class! Begin! Buy some paints!" we often sit on the fence. We pace the room instead of writing. We scrub the bathtub five times instead of crafting our jewelry. We wash the car, answer untold numbers of mindless e-mails, make soup, watch TV, or clean out the garage instead of doing our art. We cry out about our lack of time for art, but then we resist it, doubting and busying ourselves out of facing off with the very thing we're dying to do.

We don't know how to get over the hurdles of beginning or continuing to work on a new piece, and we beat ourselves up for procrastinating or not trying.

But here's the truth of art in our time: We've got to get past a lot of nasty American cultural crap that stands in the way of giving ourselves permission to lean our full body weight in the direction of our art. We have to silence the voices that want immediate money, success, or celebrity—instant results, in other words—and keep them away from our creative efforts.

Loving our art is reason enough for doing it. We don't have to explain, we don't have to justify. As Paulo Coelho writes in *The Alchemist*, "No reason is needed for loving."

We learn to answer the artistic call just because it's calling us, and when we do that, we can courageously let it lead us down the path of our well-loved, expressive creativity.

How on God's Green Earth Do I Answer "The Call"?

So, let's talk philosophy for a moment. What exactly am I talking about when I say, "Answer the artist's call"? The artist's call is simple. It's what your heart is asking you to do. It's the creative thing that's calling to you to try, to do, to write down, to paint, to craft, to build, to make, or to invent.

Know this first—right now—before you get mad at yourself for not getting this quickly enough: We are unpracticed at answering the call from the heart.

What we are good at is feeding immediate needs. Our entire sales culture is based on the knee-jerk reaction of fixing, filling, or ending some condition or circumstance for an immediate rectification. We do what Caroline Myss describes in her brilliant work, *The Anatomy of the Spirit*: When our heart calls us to do something we need to do, and our head can't figure out how, we send our *will* into addictions to mask the call. We blot it out. We cover it up with food, or drugs, or sex, or shopping, or overwork, or too much TV, or anything else we can get our hands on.

We don't sit in the question, or open it up and look at the unsolved thing on the table, or turn the quandary over in our palms until we feel its dimensions. We try to get it *off* the table as soon as it threatens to appear. We are not schooled in listening.

But know this: We can become schooled in listening. We can learn to hear what's being asked of us artistically, and then learn the courage that lets us take the first, then the second, and the third steps on our artist's path.

And, better yet, we can train ourselves to walk a path that has no path—one that requires us to blaze it.

Emerson said it as simply as anyone ever did: "There is a

guidance for each of us, and by lowly listening, we shall hear the right word."

Living as an Artist Will Absolutely Test You.

Art, in the daily working of it—in the management of our time, our life pressures, our work ethics, our need for motivation and support—is not at all a romantic, star-studded journey. In fact, it often feels like an uphill character-development battle just to get ourselves to our workbench, our sculpting studio, our easel, or our acting class.

There are boatloads of things to distract us, and no signposts along the way telling us which direction to go. We're pressed for time anyway, and usually money, too, so when we get an inspired idea that pushes at us to make art, we often get stalled and scared and drop the ball right at our inspiration point. We live between the pull of something that wants to be created from within us and the terror of what authentic action will mean to our precariously balanced work, family, and relationship lives.

We buy into all kinds of propaganda, from thinking that the only way we can pursue our art with passion is to do it full-time and have someone else support us, to believing that living as a "starving artist" will propel us to work.

And none of that works. That fear-induced, banging-around-in-the-brain argument we have with ourselves just stalls us, and contributes to nothing good. *Poverty and art? Not good. All day long at a job I hate and no art? Soul-killing. Years of going from job to job in fields I have no love for? I want to be off the planet.*

When we're stuck between ideas and action, we end up feeling paralyzed and depressed, running nasty dialogues in our head, and then blaming ourselves for our lack of movement.

And here's the thing: We don't need to go down that spinning, going-nowhere road ever again. With the application of a few simple premises and a few easy-to-manage tools, we can give up that soul-killing, frozen-in-our-tracks conversation forever. We can beat back our panic and give ourselves—and the world—what we really, really want. That is, the amazing gift of our art.

And all we need to do to get there is show up and apply a few simple-to-learn skills.

Inspiration Is Not Enough.

I love the word *inspiration*. It means "divine guidance," or "the influence of God or a god." It's the biblical parable of the talents, to build on the gifts we're given—or, as the poet Mary Oliver so aptly put it, "What will you do with your one wild and precious life?"

But inspiration alone will leave us flat.

I once told my crazy family doctor, many years ago, that

my husband had just edited an anthology of short stories and the book was being published. "I've written a book, too," the doctor said proudly. "Really?" I said. He looked me straight in the eye and tapped his finger to his brain. "It's all in here," he said, with a mocking smile.

And there it is—the heart of what delineates the artist from the dreamer; the difference between the servant of art who nourishes her talents and applies them versus the one who buries them or never lets them see the light of day.

The point of artistry is to get it *out* of our head and heart and into the world. It's about doing something concrete with our inspiration. It's about actually sitting down and creating.

It's not about talking about it, dreaming about it, blogging about it, tweeting about it, selling it, journaling on it, or angst-ing over it. It's about *making* it.

The term *working artist* should not refer to the amount of money made at the practice. It is more aptly a description of the person who shows up and does the work—day in, day out, year in, year out.

You Can Learn to Become a Healthy Artist.

When no one is clamoring for our artistic efforts—or when we feel our society's handprints on our back, chomping at the bit for monetary and success outcomes—it's often hard for us to get our mind around the concept of work-for-its-own-sake. We don't know how to give ourselves time to explore. We don't know how to develop steady work habits when there are no assured outcomes. We're shitty at working for the long-term payoff, the process-oriented joys.

We have mythologized art so severely in our culture that we don't know how to *learn* to become an artist. We miss the "becoming" part, having been duped into thinking that being one is just gifted to us, like being tapped on the shoulder by a fairy godmother and then being "discovered."

So, it's not by accident that artists in our country have success, money, addiction, and stability issues. We don't, as a society, offer guidance on how to acquire the skills, the work habits, the supports, and the diligence necessary to live healthily with our creative gifts.

But here's the truth: We can *learn* those skills.

That is the most pertinent theme of this book. That being an artist means *learning how to become one.*

We don't have to be gifted to the earth as a fully formed artisan or have a grandmother's trust fund to live off of. We don't have to be an instant success or even know what we're doing when we begin.

Just like everything else in life (e.g., learning a language, cooking, driving, building strong relationships) we can learn the skills of being an artist and *apply* them to become a well-balanced and a healthy one. And that, for most of us, is really, really good news.

Nourish Your Artistic "Space."

We must, as artists, nourish the creative space around us. So, what the hell does "nourish the space" mean? It means we have to have breathing room around us or we won't be able to focus on our creativity.

Our creative voices are like kids: They need a stable environment to learn well. They can't learn, grow, or explore when there's no money to keep the lights on and the house is falling down.

Contrary to the iconic tortured-artist image we've fostered in our time, we artists don't do well when everything is tanking and there's not enough money for food. We're sensitive creatures and we feel everything on an intense wavelength.

Suffering, it turns out, is not good for us. It's like running too much electricity through already-delicate circuits.

When we're suffering, we're distracted and we don't trust ourselves. We're not free enough in our heart to create well because we're barely making it through the day. We're angst-ridden and pissy, worried and afraid—not a great emotional space for opening up to anything.

So, we have to put the supports under our soul and body that allow us to move with some peace in the world. We must do it as an act of artistic strength and wisdom. That means—if we're not independently wealthy, which most of us are not— we have to have some means of supporting ourselves, some way to create stability in our life. We have to have a way to keep poverty at bay so we can do our art without angst. We can bellyache all we want about the hours a job may take from our art, but the truth is, suffering and struggling sucks up way more hours than a self-sustaining job ever does.

Supporting ourselves gives us a real and genuine chance with our art: It nourishes the space around us so there's plenty of breathing room to invent art. And that's what we're after.

2:
GET A DAY JOB

Get a Day Job.

You're going to hate this.

So, just know you're going to hate this and read along anyway.

If you need to support yourself in the world and you need money to live (and your art's not providing it), then you've got to get a day job.

You can bullshit yourself all day long about it, but if you really, truly, want to make art and give yourself room to keep making art, you've got to have a mechanism for supporting yourself over the long term with dignity and self-sufficiency. That mechanism is called a day job.

My loving suggestion is to get one that you can stand.

Most of us artists have all kinds of gifts, so when we're looking for something to do that pays the rent *now* while our art is growing, we should not automatically assume we have to do something that we hate.

The first revelation I had when I saddled up and got the courage to go to a professional acting class was that everyone else was exactly like me. They had relationships, obligations, bills, rent to pay, and they had to support themselves at some kind of job in order to fund their acting. There was nothing special about me or my circumstances.

So, learn this now: All of us have to work to fund what we love. In some way, shape, or form, every *real* artist must give over his or her labor to fund their art.

Most days, it's going to take all of our bravery, strength, and audacity, and many days, every last ounce of our physical and spiritual energy to do our art. So, we cannot—repeat, *cannot*—be spending huge chunks of our time worrying about whether we can scrape together the rent money, pay for groceries, or afford a doctor when we've got bronchitis and still expect to have mental bandwidth for art and inspiration. It's just not going to happen.

Accept this now: A job will give you the support you need to create. In plain English, that means that for almost all of us, being a "real artist" means getting and keeping a day job.

Be Willing to Be Good at More than One Thing.

The best advice I can offer about finding a day job that works for your artist life is to be willing to see it through the lens of being good at more than one thing.

As artists we are often talented at many things already. If we can sing, we might also be able to cook, design, play guitar, or paint. If we can draw, we might also be able to write, landscape, or build houses.

The point is to look to these talents first, as we're choosing our day job, or as we're moving from a job we can't stand to one that will really sustain us, emotionally and financially.

When I was a younger artist, I fell into a terrible pit with my day jobs. I kept moving from one miserable job to another, jumping frying-pan-into-the-fire to the next one with my only thought being: "How much money can I make?" I hated my work life so much that my weeks took on an awful, schizophrenic sensation of intense pleasure with my husband on evenings and weekends, and depressing misery as the hour for my next workday approached. This setup will not work to fund an artistic life.

So, when I say, "Get a day job you can stand," I'm dead serious. You will have to put some effort into finding it, and it will take some time away from your art for a little while to explore what you can do to support yourself in a way that you will feel okay or even good about.

I cannot say this strongly enough: If you hate your job or the field you make money in, you must spend the time and effort to find something you can do that you're at peace with, or you will always be suffering. And suffering, as we said before, just sucks up all the air in the room that we need for making art.

A List to Live By.

Once, when I was dangling precariously by a depressive thread and had no idea how to end the wretchedness of my going-nowhere day jobs, a friend gave me some really good advice.

He said, "Make a list of everything you're good at and everything you love. Put a copy on your fridge, on your mirror, and on your closet door. Look at it every day for at least three months."

And I thought, *What good is that going to do? I already know I love to eat, cook, shop, sing, paint, act, write—and that and 25 cents will get me a spot selling myself on some corner! Who's going to pay me to do what I love?*

But I did the exercise anyway. And over time, what happened was I began to pay attention to more of my talents. I began to listen for opportunities that I wouldn't have paid attention to before. I started changing my attitude and my approach.

I ended up selling a brownie recipe to Trader Joe's. I got asked to write a couple of nonunion TV scripts. I got paid to do some personal chef work. And though none of those things became my main gig, it opened me up to what I can do, and what I like to do, and that it's possible to support myself at something I actually feel good about. A door opened up inside me.

The "Good People" Day Job.

There are two kinds of day jobs. The first one I call the "Good People" day job.

This is the kind of job that is populated by good people who are kind to you and for whom you provide a worthy service. The job is not necessarily something you would search out on your must-have interest list, but the work is pleasant enough, and the people are genuine and kindhearted.

The "Good People" day job can work very well for us artists, as long as we're making enough money to reasonably cover our expenses.

What does "reasonably cover expenses" mean? It means you can pay for your housing, transportation, food, drugstore items, clothes, medical care, some entertainment, a bit of savings, an emergency fund, your art supplies, and a yearly vacation. In other words, it's a job that will fund your life and keep you from suffering.

The criteria for a "Good People" day job is simple: The place pays you a decent living wage, they treat you well, they're kind, there is a sense of community at work that's easy on the soul, and generally speaking, there's a spirit of contentment around your workplace.

Although every workplace will have its moments, this is not a high-pressure, backbiting, bickering environment. These people are responsible, amenable, and when you say you have to leave at the last minute before a big project deadline because your father died, they send you out the door immediately with condolences, good wishes, and no hesitation.

While you may be at the reception desk or coordinating the office, you can come to work knowing you will be respected and treated well. This is good foundation upon which to build an artistic life. Think: no drama.

That said, this kind of job can work on our artistic soul and turn sour if we're not connected to an ethic of being of service. The way I learned to do this was to say to myself, *Okay, this job is barely using 10 percent of my gifts. But that 10 percent is incredibly valuable to the people I'm giving it to. If I just show up to be of service here, I'll learn that same work ethic with my art.*

It involves a kind of worker humility to abide by this perspective, an understanding that we are only a worker among workers, each with our unique interests and needs, each offering our labor to support our life choices.

Put simply, we want to respect our workplace. Don't go telling your boss or your workmates that this is just a "nothing" day job for you and that as soon as you make it big, you'll be out the door. No one likes to be used. Instead, let them in on your slow and steady approach to exploring your creativity, and thank them for the supports they provide to your life and your art. They will feel like they're doing something monumental and important, even if you're a writer who's just starting to put pen to page or a sculptor who has barely begun to sculpt. Everyone loves to be appreciated.

And when your "Good People" boss and workmates know they're contributing to your passions, it will make their work more meaningful, too.

The "Secondary Arts" Day Job.

The other kind of day job is called the "Secondary Arts" day job.

This is the kind of job that's related to things you love, things that might be second or third down on the list of your most passionate artistic interests, but things to which you feel very connected just the same.

Although the "Secondary Arts" day job isn't on the top of the list of our most ardent artistic interests, it is still wholly related to things we enjoy and to things that come easily to us.

It may not pay as much as a mainstream "Good People" job, so the importance of earning enough and living within our means heightens dramatically here. Our object is no drama in our self-sustaining supports, particularly with money.

If we choose a "Secondary Arts" job, we absolutely have to employ the same criteria we did in the "Good People" job with regard to covering our expenses. We can't say, "Oh, terrific! I'll be a part-time stage manager making $16,000 a year so I can be close to the theater," and still expect to fund a life. Things cost what they cost. And though we can make conscious choices to live on less—choices that buy us artistic time—we still have to provide for all the things we need to live well, without struggle. We all know what we're talking about here: rent, food, clothes, savings, medical care—all of it. We cannot expect to suffer in poverty and make amazing art. It just won't work.

In my own life, it took years for me to move from the

difficult jobs I was doing to a "Secondary Arts" job. It felt like such a heavy and hard transition that I likened it to moving an ocean liner from south to north in the middle of a headwind. I had been grant writing for years, and my clients were running up big deficits and then dumping the pressure on me, and it made me completely miserable. It was not a "Good People" job (even though it seemed so, given the causes), because the people were all revved up on desperation and adrenaline.

So, we don't want to trap ourselves into believing that a difficult job is a "Good People" job or a "Secondary Arts" job just because the cause is noble. We don't want to pretend that underpaying, frantic, or mean-spirited employers are okay for our support system just because they engage in some task we philosophically believe in.

We've got to look at this in a holistic way. It's like being in a relationship: We can't pretend the partnership works because the sex is good when there's unkindness, meanness, or no respect or ethics in it.

In other words, we don't stay in a job for the money or the cause when the environment generates misery. We have to have peace in our day-job life or we won't have room in our head and heart for our art. It's that simple.

Do Well, in Every Arena of Your Life.

Because we're learning how to do two things at once—support ourselves and live as artists—we can sometimes miss the fact that there are opportunities at our day jobs that we can reach for.

Meaning, just because we're artists doesn't mean we can't excel at our day jobs. Excelling anywhere—even on the basketball court at lunch or cooking dinner in our own kitchen—helps our art. Wherever we build self-esteem in our life translates directly to self-worth and confidence in our creative work.

Several years ago I helped a friend negotiate a full-time salary and benefits at a real estate development office in which she had gotten a temp job. She had been hanging back, thinking that she didn't deserve a real job offer because she was an actress and had to leave occasionally from work for auditions. When I pointed out that other people left during the day for dentist appointments, kids' Little League games or dance contests, or a doctor's appointment for their aging mom, she got it.

The thing was, she was so skilled so quickly that the associate manager told the boss that if they didn't hire my friend, she would leave her managerial post. My friend had leveraging power as a worker, and she needed to use it to better her life and fund her artistry. She did, and got a very nice salary and full benefits.

The point is this: Our work is not less valuable just because we have another thrust in our life that's driving us. We should not apologize for being artists by hanging back in our day jobs and taking scraps for positions or salaries. We can ask for what we need, show up as reliable and responsible workers, *and* fund what's meaningful to us—our creative life.

So, don't be afraid to ask for a promotion or benefits when negotiating for a job that supports you. Don't sit at the reception desk for another year because you're afraid that the project coordinator job will drain you. Busy, accomplished people do more in life, so trust that you can excel in multiple areas and still do your art. Know that the skills of managing time well are learned (we will talk about them shortly), and do your best, even at your day job.

Don't Bite the Hand that Feeds You.

Once, a musician friend of mine told me something her clergyman told her. He said, "Wouldn't you love for someone to come along and pay your bills, buy your food, and support you while you do your art?" "Yes!" she said. "Great," he replied. "That person is your boss."

And that speaks to how to behave when we're in the day job workplace; to what our ethics should be. I used to go to a spiritual center in Los Angeles, and the minister there said a profound thing. He said, "If you're dying for a big, creative job and you're not fully inhabiting the job you have now, how are you going to develop the capacity for the big one?"

For me, "fully inhabiting" my jobs meant I had to see that even if I felt I was only using a few of my minor gifts there, my labor was of genuine service, and I could learn to be humble and grateful for the money I earned to support myself and my art. In other words, I had to learn to show up for work with a good attitude and some thankfulness for having my bills paid.

So, even if you have to stand in front of your office's bathroom mirror 10 times a day and chant, "Make me of service! Make me willing to show up!" then do it. Show up with ethics and a good attitude, knowing that your boss is directly supporting your art, and see how your creativity flourishes.

Stop Complaining and Take Some Action.

The humility of learning to be grateful for my day jobs made me more honest about the fact that, even though a lot of the angst in my work was not of my doing, I was still just complaining; I wasn't taking the steps necessary to help change my day job to something I liked or felt enriched by.

For years I had been playing long shots to fund my artwork, leveraging money and praying for instant, big-time triumphs. I was angry when there were no quick-fix miracle successes to get me out of less fulfilling work and I took out that bitterness on my job situations. I wasn't being remotely truthful about the genuine efforts I needed to make to get a sustaining job that I liked. It was easier to just complain and stay stuck.

One day, I was bitching about one of my grant clients— how they had not even thanked me when a big proposal I wrote got funded—and my friend said, "Look, you've hated this work for years. When are you going to stop moaning and do something about it?"

And that woke me up.

I didn't even realize how stuck I was. Action was the only thing that was going to change my life, and I had to get serious about my efforts to change things. I couldn't keep standing on the sidelines of my day-job life, praying that one of my art projects was going to rescue me in instantaneous glory. I had to woman-up and give this problem some of my sweat and blood.

Then, I did: I moved that 10-ton ship-trajectory of dissatisfaction, and started teaching yoga instead of grant writing. It took a year to figure out that teaching yoga was going to do it. I had to investigate; I had to research. I had legwork to do. I tried finding work in several arenas—private school instructor, substitute teacher, chef, fitness instructor, technical writer—and it took all of that research and time to finally get to what was going to work.

But I still had more changes to make. I had to learn to live on less money, to live on cash and not credit. I had to give up grandiosity and instant-success thinking, and fully fund every artistic thing that I birthed. I wanted absolutely no money pressure for myself; no more boxing myself in, no more having to do work that I didn't like or couldn't stand to get myself out of a financial hole.

It took over a year to build a yoga practice, to start making a living beyond bare sustenance. But I did it. And—surprise, surprise—it turns out that I *love* teaching yoga, and I have never once looked back to my old life. I'm happy now, my art is supported, I'm supported, and so is my relationship. I have balance, and I can breathe for the first time in my adult life.

That's what we want: room in our spirit, mind, and daily life to do our artwork with no crazy money hardship, no low-level or awful drama, and no back-to-the-wall, pressure-cooker employee situations blotting out our creative voice.

So, explore. Use your interest list to look under every rock that's in your talent yard. Put yourself out there in several different arenas of your interests. Make real and honest efforts. Be patient. Then wait to see what pops.

A day job with good people or a day job that's on your loved list—either way, make the effort to support yourself with something your soul can live with. Then, watch as your art begins to blossom before your eyes.

Learn This Now: Slow, Steady Steps Are Better than All-or-Nothing Events.

Let me relieve you of a notion that has been erroneously hammered into our heads in the last 20 years of cosmica-rama, New Age hype. That is, the "Do what you love and the money will follow" myth.

This is the nastiest lie that ever hit the good, hard earth—which is exactly where our feet need to be planted if we ever hope to get any damned artwork done. "Do what you love and the money will follow" has encouraged a whole generation of artists to put the cart before the horse—that is, to borrow and run up debt against our art as a way of supposedly kick-starting the process of "doing what we love." And it doesn't work.

Let me tell you what happens when we do that. When we put ourselves in the hole to get our art gallery out of our garage, or to stock up on silver for our jewelry business, or to fund a first music CD that's supposed to be our salvation from any more day jobs (as I did), we put enormous pressure on our projects to succeed right out of the gate. And our budding artwork can't stand the strain.

Think: We're raising our art as we would raise a child, to stand on its own two feet. When we buy ourselves stuff that we can't yet afford—even stuff we think we "need" for our artwork—we end up desperate to have our newly launched art *sell* the minute it hits the market. Why? Because we're behind the eight ball, we're borrowing up to our eyeballs, and we need our work to pay off *now*. We need a bailout— and fast. And that kind of pressure gives our work no normal growth arc, no natural development process. It's like asking a two-year-old to do eight-year-old math.

And here's the kicker: *Our desperation often makes us fail.* Even a little bit of that kind of money pressure can plunge us into panic and worry and make our projects tank.

The same thing happens when we're scraping by on no job and no cash, barely getting by and hitting up our parents to pay our rent every month. It's debilitating as adults not to be able to support ourselves, and it dings our artistic confidence in a serious, downward-spiral descent.

"Do what you love and the money will follow" really means this: Do something that you enjoy, get paid for it, *live within your means*, and build on that.

Need new headshots for your acting auditions? Great—*save* for them. Your agent's not going to die if you wait three months to get them. Need new canvasses and can't afford them? Great. Save until you can afford them. Or go to the thrift store and find old paintings for $3 and paint over them. Be inventive, be creative, and keep the pressure off your back.

Trust me, you do not want to put the cart before the horse or you will flatten all the space you have in your heart for creative exploration. It will seep out like air from a deflated balloon and all that you will have left in its place is dread and worry.

And don't assume that because you have to be inventive financially, you are cutting yourself off from the grace of your artistry. Remember that Jackson Pollock painted his drip paintings with buckets of cheap and free house paint, and his black, white, and tan-colored hues became the foundation of his signature style.

The point is, we artists need to do what we need to do to stay solvent and strong. No over-the-top dive-ins that put us behind the eight ball. No pressure-cooker nightmares that block our inspiration and tank our emotional well-being. Slow, steady steps must be our motto.

3:

MAKE PEACE WITH YOUR MONEY

Money Clarity Buys You Time.

One of the most ridiculous things we do to ourselves as artists is to check out on our money. We say, "Oh, I'm an artist—I'm no good with keeping track of cash." Or "I'm a train wreck with numbers. I'm a creative type."

And that, all by itself, can send our artistic life down the river.

When we engage in that kind of nonsense, we are missing the most salient point of what clarity in our finances buys us. Clarity buys us *time*. The more we're clear about what we have and what we need to spend on bills, daily needs (e.g., food and fuel), and simple savings (for car repairs, a vacation, etc.), the more we can buy ourselves freedom.

When we know what it costs us to live, we can consciously choose to downsize for a cause. That cause, in our case, is more time for our art. That's what we're always crying out for, and it's why we resist getting a day job. So, if we want more freedom, we have to get more clarity. And that means we have to know what we spend and what we need.

Let me give you an example. When I finally got a clear plan for my expenses and began using a simple mechanism to keep track of my daily spending, I chose to downsize so

I could write my first book. I chose a job that paid me less, and one that I loved more, which let me have lots of hours during the week to write. I downsized my monthly spending by about $500 a month to buy myself time, and it freed me up to do my art. Did I care that I only had $40 or $50 a month for clothes instead of $100 or $150, or $25 for beauty supplies instead of $80? No. Did I care that I stopped being able to splurge at the swanky grocery store and instead began shopping at local discounters? No. Because the freedom I felt having more art time far outweighed the pleasure of $23-per-pound organic beef or a $100 blouse.

For all the years I was just getting by, having no clear plan and spending randomly, I was tied paycheck to paycheck. I spent everything I had, had no savings, and ran up debt on my art projects and living expenses besides. And that meant I could not step back from the day-job world at all. I felt trapped by my vague and wishy-washy finances, and by my mounting money pressure. It wasn't a fun feeling, by a long shot. And it didn't get better until I made the effort to work out a simple plan to live on my cash income.

The point is, we don't want to slit our own throat by engaging in the smokescreen of the "I'm no good with numbers" conversation. It will just bring us pain and suffering. And we know now that suffering is no good for artists.

Want more time for art? Great. Then get more clarity. Plan a little. Live within your means. Don't argue, fuss, or fight about it with yourself. Make it simple, clear, and easy, and be willing to make that change.

That's the way it works. Get clear, get willing, take the money pressure out of your life, and your art world will fill up with fresh air and freedom.

Anyone Can Add.

There's another conspicuous detail that we often bowl over in our artist attempts to check out on our finances. It's an easy truth. That is, a monthly living expense plan is based on *simple addition*. Add, subtract, then add and subtract. Okay, so maybe we're not hip to the superfund investment world of Wall Street types or E★TRADE business gurus. Fine. But we don't need that expertise to be good at our own finances. The only skills we need are addition, subtraction, and *willingness*.

So, I invite you to check the creative money prejudice you've been holding against yourself at the door right now. Stop saying—out loud or to yourself—that you're no good with managing money. Stop saying you can't handle numbers. Be willing to see something else—something that's better and more supportive of the life you want to lead.

That means, even for this one moment, you'll be willing to see that clarity in your finances will assist you in your artist's life, will buy you time, and—just like investing the energy to get a day job you can live with—will be worth the effort.

This chapter details a simple structure to help you create a money plan that, step by step, will realistically support your artist's life month to month. Don't worry—it's simple and easy on the soul. Use it if you like, or use something else, but get yourself a plan *of some kind.*

Having a strong yet flexible structure for monthly needs is the foundation for any artist who wants to get serious about his or her work. It's a necessary bedrock tool for living the life we really want to live. So, don't check out. Keep reading, and know that this chapter is written for artists—for *you*—and not for businesspeople.

It's based on simple addition, and anyone can do it.

Don't Use Credit Cards to Fund Your Life.

Learning to live as a healthy artist means we have to give up the stuff that's not working for us anymore. Pressure that blocks our creativity, jobs that promote struggling or misery, money drama, underearning—all of these fall into the "unhealthy" category. This stuff just won't serve us over time. And debt contributes to each one of them.

Debt pressure does not work in the artist's life. What debt does is cut off the very choices we're dying to make for ourselves, such as more time for art, less money pressure, and more freedom to explore. Debt—even a little bit of it—makes a mess of our well-being, blocks our freedom to work without pressure, and damages our future. It spins nasty webs of manic-depressive thinking, as we pray for a miracle to rescue us from the mess we've made of our finances, and then sinks us ever-deeper into despondency and desperation over the fact that we're living to pay off our creditors.

When we engage in debt, we cut off our choices. It blocks our courage to leave a job we hate, because our sole concern is our bottom line and not our emotional well-being. And because we're often adding to our debt, and living paycheck to paycheck besides, that makes us want to rebel and run up more debt, using even more credit to buy ourselves a dinner out, an expensive suit, or a weekend away to give ourselves a "break" from the pressure.

Debt blocks opportunities that might be meaningful to us, too, such as downsizing our expenses so we can write a book, or living on less to take a painting residency in South America or a job teaching music for three months in a Nepalese school.

It's a downward spiral with debt in the picture. There's not one good thing that comes from debt pressure and we all know it. And though debt is a pressure cooker for everyone, it's worse for us artists. We need breathing room, and debt gives us none. We have to admit the truth: A life funded by debt will not work for the artist.

That's why a monthly spending plan for living on our cash income is so important for us. When we learn to live within our means—simply and easily—we're available to the creative opportunities that we're working so hard to find for ourselves. We're pliable, open, and receptive, and not fearful or rigid.

So, try with all your might to accept this now: Credit cards and borrowing are death traps for the artist. The best thing we can do for ourselves is to get a day job we can live with, live on what we earn, and slowly pay off any debt we owe without adding to it.

When we give ourselves the dignity of a pressure-free environment to build and grow our creativity, we flourish. When we don't, we don't.

Map Out What It Costs You to Live.

We're going to get good and practical here. If this approach is going to help you in your artist's life at all, it's got to be hands-on and it's got to be easy. The good news is, what I'm about to share with you is both. It's called a personal spending plan—not a budget—because you get to choose your own priorities for spending.

Here's what you're going to do. You're going to divide your expenses into two categories: Bills and Daily Needs.

Bills are exactly what they sound like: amounts you have to pay each month, on a regular basis, billed out by a service provider. Rent. Mortgage. Health insurance. Home or renter's insurance. Phone bills. Cable. Netflix. Credit card payments. Gym membership. Newspaper subscriptions. Whatever it is that you pay out as a bill, list it.

Then, when you're done with that, make a *short* list on another sheet of all the things you need for Daily Needs. Food.

Fuel. Drugstore. Beauty or personal products. Dry cleaning. Haircuts. Household. Clothes. Postage. Copays. Add a category for any services you get on a regular basis, such as massage or acupuncture. Add childcare payments or kid's clothing allotments if you've got kids. Since these amounts are not set by a service provider as bills are, just ballpark and guess what you think you use or need in a month.

Then think about all of the things you need annually, such as car repairs, unexpected medical expenses, family trips, vacation money, kids' camps, Christmas and holiday money. Ballpark what you need in each category and average those amounts by 12 months. Don't forget simple annual bills, such as your DMV renewal, website hosting costs, business license, sales tax, or other art-income tax you may need to put aside. List all these amounts in a simple format. Here is a specific example:

BILLS	
Rent	1,295.00
Water, gas & electric	55.00
Health insurance	455.00
Cell phone	155.12
Car insurance	129.19
Studio share rent	144.13
Art portfolio website	12.00
Renter's insurance	15.99
Student loan	230.00
	$2,491.43

DAILY NEEDS	
Food (groceries)	390.00
Fuel	240.00
Drugstore	25.00
Beauty/personal	25.00
House supplies	20.00
Laundry	20.00
Dry cleaners	25.00
Clothes	45.00
Art supplies	75.00
Eating out/entertainment	75.00
Extra	25.00
	$965.00
SAVINGS NEEDS	
Healthy reserve (emergencies)	45.00
Short-term savings	75.00
Christmas	35.00
Vacation/travel	50.00
Family visits	45.00
	$250.00
TOTAL EXPENSES	**$3,706.43**

Notice that the example is a relatively simple expense list, and still, the total is $3,706.43—or about a $4,700-per-month salary before taxes. There will be all kinds of variables for your own monthly plan; for instance, does your employer cover your health insurance costs? If so, you can nix that from your list. Do you have the ability to take some retirement money out pretax? If so, then do it. Do you need to account for credit card payments, or additional costs, such as child-care? Then add them. Do you live in a city and use public transit instead of keeping a car? Then make that adjustment. Keep the categories simple. No more than 10 to 12 categories in the Daily Needs area. (You'll find out why in a minute when we discuss how to work the spending plan.)

Cut Expenses to Buy Yourself Freedom.

For most artists, this simple listing of what it costs us to live is a serious wake-up call. It typically knocks us over to notice how much money is needed to fund our life—even a financially simple one. And since we're usually mindlessly spending over and above what we earn without any clarity at all, the pressure increases for us. When we do that—when we overspend with no guidelines or clarity—we are cementing ourselves to a life of living paycheck to paycheck; to stress, to angst, and to the have-to pressure of staying in jobs we don't like or want. And that makes us resentful, angry, helpless, and desperate. And it kills our artistic drive, too.

But staying stuck in our resentment and panic over our own financial situation will get us nowhere. Feeling put-upon will help us not one bit. Nor will putting our head in the sand and trying to grind through our financial situation blindly. We have to stand up and take responsibility for ourselves if anything is ever going to change for the better financially, and therefore, artistically. And the only thing that's going to work is to take real and concrete action to live within our means.

It's very much our job to support ourselves. It's not our parents' job, or our ex-partner's, or our society's (e.g., if we're hanging out living on student loans or unemployment for years on end). It's our responsibility to look clearly at what it *really* costs us to live, and fund that for ourselves. We have to support ourselves *and* do our art. That's our job as adults.

That doesn't mean that there aren't endless creative ways to reduce expenses and therefore give ourselves more freedom to do art. There are thousands of ways to make our living expenses easier to manage should we choose to apply them.

The simplest way, particularly if we're already in debt, is to look at areas we can cut. The cable, the home phone, and the credit card are the most obvious and the easiest bills to downsize. Even cutting the "small" expenses, like newspaper and magazine subscriptions, and daily coffee bar purchases, can make a huge dent in saving cash that creates more money for art. In our house, we cut the cable ($120 per month) and now use the public library's free DVDs along with a Netflix streaming subscription for $7.99 per month. That money now funds our travel account: expenses we used to put on credit cards.

Downsizing insurance for a cheaper plan for home, car, or renter's plans, sharing an art studio, getting rid of the home phone, getting a roommate, renting a room in your house on airbnb.com or other shared home sites—all of these are simple ways to generate some more cash and pay down debt or add to your income.

If you need more detailed guidance on how to downsize without pain, feel free to read my first book, *The Debt-Free Spending Plan,* available on all the usual sites (for about $10), and in libraries across the country. The book's plan gives you step-by-step instruction on how to craft a monthly spending plan that covers all of your needs, with five-minute-a-day management tools. It's based on simple addition, and is designed for the eight-year-old in us who froze up in math class. I particularly recommend reading this book if you are under the pressure of serious debt, as I was. (Chapters 1 to 3 explain the plan, and chapters 5 and 9 show you how to downsize without self-deprivation to create more freedom in your money life. These chapters also detail how to keep simple records for your tax-deductible artist expenses.)

In just a moment I'll show you how to work your spending plan on a daily basis in a hands-on, practical way. For now though, just take a moment or two and make your list of Bills, Daily Needs, and Savings, then begin to think about where you can downsize to free up cash. Use the format shown in the example and list everything you'll need to spend in a month. Make it simple and not complex. We will come back to this list in a minute or two.

Beyond creative approaches to downsizing Bills and Daily Needs, there are amazing ways to fund the freedom that you crave. I have a friend who plays violin on a cruise ship for four months a year, and works on his art the other eight. Another friend rents out her inherited house and lives in a small apartment in a less expensive town, so she can choreograph and teach dance. Another acquaintance is a personal chef in a huge home, with her own private cottage, which frees her up to write for half the day.

And plenty of artists I know—particularly those with families—have professional day jobs with hours they can massage to allow for art: realtors, home health aides, teachers, fitness professionals, gardeners, part-time social workers, insurance agents, nutritionists, floral arrangers, counselors, and more. So, don't limit yourself just because you have bills to pay or a family to support. Even if you're in debt, you can stop the roller coaster of money madness by taking a few simple money clarity steps that will allow you to start building a solid art life.

Start Now.

The sooner we start getting clarity with our money, the sooner we stop feeling trapped or pressed into a corner by our life. And the more readily we find clarity, the more room we make for our creative ventures.

Usually the reason we artists don't look deeply into our finances is we're afraid that if we do, we'll never have another fulfilled want or desire for the rest of our life. So, I'm going to ask you to borrow my faith on this as I encourage you to get clarity with your money. What I know from my own experience is that when I was running up debt and working in I-hate-my-day-job spurts, I was constantly emotionally upset and sometimes even desperate. I took money risks that put me even farther behind the eight ball, which left me more stuck in work situations that tried my soul. I had no idea what it cost me to live, and no idea what I needed should I choose to live a simpler life to fund my art.

But when I got clarity, I *chose* to stop hoarding groceries, stop overspending on gifts, and stop spending mindlessly at the discount store. I *chose* to get rid of the cable and fund my art supplies. I stopped buying tea at the groovy coffee bar and saved myself enough for a travel fund. I began spending very small amounts on drugstore items, food, clothes, bodywork, Christmas presents, house supplies, and more—and that bought me freedom from having to work so much. It meant that I had to be thoughtful about what I was spending—sure—but after about three months, I got the hang of it. I came to understand that every mindless purchase stole time from my art, robbed money from something that might be more meaningful to me (e.g., a vacation with my husband), and took the life out of my creativity.

The action of learning to live within my means has changed absolutely everything: It has allowed me to fully turn my attention to art. I never, ever could have done that without the clarity I now have with my money.

So, don't wait to get money clarity. Start now and start simply. Know that every dime that comes into alignment with your true goals brings your life that much closer to happiness. Money does not have to run you. Master your money, and you'll begin mastering your art.

I firmly believe that, I have lived it, and I know it to be true.

Manage Your Money with Simple Tools.

If you're using the simple outline of the spending plan I've just described, then you'll need a way to manage that money monthly and daily. We can't just hope we'll live within the amounts we set out each month. That just won't work. And we can't wait until *after* we've spent money to settle up: That's too late. We have to know what we have *before* we spend it, so we always live within the amounts we set out in each category.

In my first book, *The Debt-Free Spending Plan,* I detail how to manage a spending plan on a two-week paycheck—meaning, though the plan is laid out as a monthly tool, paychecks are most likely coming in every two weeks, so we have to have a way of working with that schedule. I offer detail on how to allocate bills to each paycheck, in a simple list I call a Bill-Paying Plan. If you get paid monthly, you won't need a Bill-Paying Plan, because you'll just pay your bills once a month when you get a check. But if you get paid every two weeks, you'll need some help allocating which bills get paid with each check. We're going to go over it here, but if you need additional help, please don't hesitate to read pages 55–58 in *The Debt-Free Spending Plan* to learn, in more detail, how to use the tools I'm offering.

If you're already living on art income that comes in at nonregular intervals, you'll want to reference the "Know When to Say When" section in this book for details specific to your variable earning schedule.

The simple how-to overview of using a Bill-Paying Plan is this: Pay your bills twice a month, with your bimonthly paycheck, with some bills assigned to your first check and the remainder assigned to your second check. In other words, once you make this plan, you'll always know when to pay each bill.

That may mean, for my plan, I have to allocate my rent and my health and car insurance to one paycheck, and pay my utilities, cell, studio, and other bills with the other paycheck. As you start to work this yourself, know that you can manage the payments any way you like, as long as you're paying on time and still have enough money for Daily Needs, such as food and fuel, in each two-week period.

I learned—surprise!—that I could call my providers and ask them to change my due dates so they worked for my Bill-Paying Plan, aligned with when my paychecks come in. Then I didn't have to struggle through two weeks of having no living expenses because I had multiple bills due.

Make it work for you. Allocate your bill-paying to each two-week check, and make sure you have enough to cover your Daily Needs as well. I try to cover all my Daily Needs in the first month's paycheck if at all possible, plus a few small

Bills, and then I fund the remainder of my Bills with my second check. That way I always know I have enough for the malleable expenses of food, fuel, drugstore, and so on. But do what works for you. The point is to have clarity about what you're paying out in Bills, and to know *exactly* what you have left to live on for Daily Needs for that pay period.

A Bill-Paying Plan from our example looks like this:

PAYCHECK 1 AUGUST 4	$1870.30
Daily Needs for month	965.00
Health insurance	455.00
Car insurance	129.19
Student loan	230.00
Art portfolio website	12.00
Renter's insurance	15.99
Water, gas & electric	55.00
	$1,862.18 (+$8.12)
PAYCHECK 2 AUGUST 18	**$1870.30**
Rent	1295.00
Cell phone	155.12
Studio share rent	144.13
Savings accounts	250.00
	$1,844.25 (+$26.05)

Note that in this instance I have a little extra, which I can add into my Daily Needs money for a little extra cushion, or put in savings money, or I can massage the numbers to make them come out even. If I don't have enough to cover all of my listed needs, then I have to downsize some of the categories to make it balance. That's the way it works. You cut when your expenses are over your cash income and then you live within the amounts you set out for yourself.

And—here's the revelation!—when you do that, you'll always get to keep the money you set aside for yourself and your artwork. You'll *stop* living to pay bills, and you'll start getting some much-coveted freedom.

Simple addition, simple balancing, simple solvency—that's all you need to get rid of money stress forever and begin building a life with art at the center.

Five Minutes a Day.

So, how do I manage my Daily Needs so I don't go over my allotted amounts? I use a simple tool I call the Magic Little Notebook. The notebook is simple: It's a list by category of what I have to spend. You can do it two ways: (1) get a 3 by 5-inch notebook from the drugstore, or (2) use the Notes function on your smartphone. Either way works fine.

And here's the brilliant part: Keeping track of what you're spending will take you no more than five minutes a day. That's right. Five minutes a day to get that vague, nasty albatross of money pressure off your artist's back—forever.

Here's what you'll do:

For each category of Daily Needs, you'll need a page—for

instance, in our example, Food $390.00 will have a page; Fuel $240.00 will have a page; Drugstore $25.00 will have a page. When you are going to spend money, pull out your notebook or your Notes app and take a look at what you have to spend. Once you make a purchase, list that purchase on the page and subtract:

ON ONE PAGE:	
Food	+390.00
8/2 Trader Joe's	-67.42
	+322.58
ON ANOTHER PAGE:	
Fuel	+240.00
8/5 Eagle gasoline	-47.13
	+192.87

The beauty of this system is, first of all, it's simple. You don't have to learn any complicated software or understand any new financial app. All you have to do is add and subtract. Its simplicity is based on one terrific thing: *You look before you spend.* If you don't have the cash, you don't buy the object.

Place all of your living expenses (the money for your Bills, your Savings allotments, and your Daily Needs) in one checking account that's just for you. If you live with a partner, get your own checking account and put into it your Daily Needs cash and the money for the Bills that you're responsible for paying. Get your own savings accounts at a credit union that charges no monthly service fees. *Don't* use the excuse of a joint account with a money-vague partner to ditch your responsibility for clarity. Get your own accounts, be clear, and be responsible.

Work with a debit card always, never credit cards. Why don't we use credit cards? Don't we want the miles? Don't we want the perks? In a perfect world—a world where we had plenty of money, no accruing debt, and no money pressure at all—sure, the convenience of credit cards would make sense. But many of us artists have had trouble with credit cards. We don't pay them off. We accrue large chunks of interest, and we end up feeling boxed in and pressured by our need to pay. Artists need the flexibility of being able to respond—not just artistically, but financially—to the creative callings that spring unbidden from our artistic soul. That means we cannot burden ourselves with extra money pressure, which is exactly what unsecured credit card debt is.

So, what happens if we're using our debit card, listing what we spend, and we go over in one category of our spending? In the normal course of a daily life, stuff is going to fall outside the lines: That's just the nature of how life shows up. So we have to be flexible. We can't be rigid or we'll end up throwing our best efforts out the window.

Let's say we allotted $9.00 this month for postage, but neglected to anticipate that we needed to mail 10 of our music CDs at $2.12 per package. Do we have to wait for another month to send them? Do we freak out and chuck the whole spending plan? *No.*

Here's what we do. We look in our other categories and

see what's there, and where we might be able to move some cash from one category to another to cover our CD-mailing expense. Is there not much to buy for the house this month? Do we already have dish soap, plastic wrap, and toilet paper? If so, then let's move some cash from that category to help fund the CD mailings. We write down each money move in our Magic Notebook so we can see it later, so we know where our money has gone. It looks like this:

ON ONE PAGE:	
Postage	+9.00
8/6 CD mailings	−21.20
	−12.20
8/6 from House	+12.20
	0.00
ON ANOTHER PAGE:	
House	+20.00
8/3 Walgreens	−3.20
	+16.80
8/6 Move to postage	−12.20
	+4.60

It's simple. Realistically, you will have to get used to how much you've allotted for each category, and it will take about three months before you get the hang of how to work your plan. For instance, I have learned that I don't want to move money from my Food or Fuel categories, since I will need that money all month long. In my other areas—such as drugstore and beauty products—I can reasonably go to the discount store once a month and get everything I need. I shop once a month and *no more* for those items, and I stay within my plan that way (and save myself a lot of unnecessary shopping, too).

For Food and Fuel I now shop once per week, dividing my allotted money by the number of Fridays in one month. I leave a little left over each week for unexpected or variable expenses, so I don't go over. Meaning, if I have $400 for my Food category and there are four Fridays, I spend a little less than $100 a week on food. That way I have money all month long for that need.

Here's one important thing about shopping and spending this way that you need to know: *Do not stock up.* Stocking up is code for overspending. Buy only what you need for one week—and I promise you it will be less than you think you need. No 24-pack chicken breasts (because they're on sale) that ding your food money for the rest of the month. When I first worked this plan myself, I realized I only needed three or four vegetables and some salad stuff each week from the produce store, and that's all I could really eat. I didn't need the vats of vegetables I had been buying, which I ended up throwing away because I couldn't eat them all before they went bad.

The point of all this is to learn to live simply, live clearly, and keep our overhead down. If we tend to freak out and go nuts with overspending in reaction to being on our new money plan, then we need some support group help. Try a group like Debtor's Anonymous, which is free and offers lots of support with overspending and money clarity issues. (Many cities have special groups just for artists, and there are phone meetings as well, for people who have scheduling issues or live far away from places where there are meetings.)

Remember that every dollar in overspending literally steals our art from us.

When we keep it simple and clear, and live within our means, we create breathing room in our life. And breathing room means more money and more time for art. And that's the whole point of this plan.

Use Whatever Works.

You may think that what I'm advocating—a small paper notebook or a list in your Notes app—is completely technologically retro. But many artists I know don't move in the tech tools world easily, and many of us have trouble with everything from Quicken to Google wallet to Mint.com. So, using tools that make us feel blocked or stymie us, or that we just resist using, isn't an effective strategy.

If we are willing to learn one of the many tech tools available for tracking spending, we usually have terrific intentions to keep our receipts entered and current, but at some early-on point we may end up getting frustrated, lost, or bored, and chuck the whole program. And then we're back where we started, in the quagmire of vagueness and being stuck.

Money tech tools also bring up the issue of time. Sometimes a program or app is just too complicated to use simply in five minutes a day, which is usually about the bandwidth we have for our finances as artists.

The trouble with all these money management tools is not that we're not bright. It's that we tend to use our difficulty figuring out the quirks of an app or program to stop us. At the first roadblock in learning one, we throw up our hands and say, "See! I'm just no good with money!" And, to be fair, sometimes our artist brain is not wired to follow what might seem intuitive to a programmer, but isn't to a creative user.

And here's the amazing kicker about tech tools: Ninety-eight percent of the apps and programs out there *won't help you.* How come? Because most are tracking tools—meaning, they help us track what we've already spent. And waiting until *after* we've spent money is too damn late! We've got to have an easy system that lets us check to see whether we have the money *before we spend it!* That's why the spending plan is different from a spending tracking device. The spending plan is a *plan for spending*, not a record of what damage we may or may not have already done.

We need to get this through our head if we're going to find any freedom at all with our money: Waiting until after we spend to look at our money is too late. We need a strong yet flexible plan that lets us know what we have to spend *before* we spend it. That's the only effective way to live within the categories we set out each month.

If you love tech tools, the best one I know of is called

www.YouNeedABudget.com. It's the easiest and most intuitive of all the apps and programs I've sorted through. But there's no need to learn it if you choose to use a small notebook or a Notes app and list your expenses on your phone.

So, what if the plan listed here—dividing Bills and Daily Needs, and using a notebook to look at your plan's simple categories before you spend—still feels too heavy for you? What if you can't possibly get your mind around it, even in its simple-list simplicity? Then make it even simpler: Allocate a few bills to pay with each paycheck, note how much you have left over, and keep a running list of what you spend from that leftover total. Have $300 left over after bills and putting aside a little bit of savings? Great. Keep a notebook and list everything you spend against the $300, and don't go over. Two weeks later, you'll do the same thing again.

The upshot is, we need something simple, something we can't check out on, and something that takes just a few minutes a day or we won't use it. That's the Magic Notebook idea. A few categories in a simple list. Easy. Based solely on addition and subtraction in a straightforward list.

To sum it all up, if technology comes easily to you, then swing out and use one of the hundreds of money apps on the market, noting that you still have to have a plan-before-you-spend strategy. If you hate technology, then just use a simple list (in a Word document or on paper), and use your Magic Notebook or a Notes app to track your daily spending. Use your debit card and never credit. That's my advice.

In the end, it doesn't matter how you do it, but you *must*

have a money plan of some kind or you'll get lost in the weeds. Keep it simple and stay *in* your creative life. That's the idea.

The Payoff.

So, why am I going into such detail to explain this way of managing money?

For one simple reason: The payoff packs a wallop. When we stop mindlessly spending, we start—humbly and simply—allocating our funds and our time, with clarity, to our art. We begin to know what we can live on, what amounts we need to put real supports under our feet, and where we can back off from the workaday world and dedicate energy, money, and time to art.

Without that clarity, we are doomed to repeat the same awful cycle that's been drummed into us since we were children about barely-making-it-artists. That is, working a day job with no art life on one pendulum swing, or slogging away at art in poverty and money desperation on the other. We have to choose the higher choice—the third choice—the one that includes *both* the need for financial supports and the need to work our artistic gifts.

There is nothing glorious about poverty. Nor is there anything grand about burying our artistic gifts in a corporate job.

Truly, even when I read books about now-famous artists who struggled on the streets of New York or Chicago or San Francisco in their early years, I am daunted by the romantic picture these tales paint of their early years in poverty. Poverty is hard. It does not spur the spirit to great heights. It's a drag on our heart and soul, our emotions and our self-worth, as well as on the well-being of our body.

Going to the other extreme and dulling ourselves in day jobs we can't stand, with no hope of building an art life, won't work either. When we block out our gifts, we will tend to be angry and agitated—with our jobs, our partners, our families, and our lives. If we're gifted, we're called. And that call will continue to eat away at us until we do something concrete with it.

The payoff of working a spending plan—or any plan that keeps us solvent and supported on our earned income—is that we give ourselves balance. And as our art grows and new opportunities appear, we're available to new choices—well-funded choices that open up into a buildable art career.

Fund the Things You Love.

When the call comes to fund our new CD, our self-published children's book, our sculpture in bronze, or our 20-foot-high collage-on-canvas, we want to be able to answer it. That means, in simple terms, we have to fund what we love.

The money plan I've detailed lets us do that. It allows us to set aside cash for the things that are meaningful to us, including art supplies. As long as we live within the categories we set out for our Bills and Daily Needs—or however we work our money plan—we get to keep the cash we set aside for art. That's our incentive for living within our means.

Put another way, we're not learning to manage our money so that we can be good little citizens and get a gold star. We're not in this to wage a campaign to improve credit scores. We need to learn to have money clarity so that we can make art without pressure. That's it. We need that kind of solvency to be fearless in the face of our own creative impulses.

Let me give you an example. I funded my first music CD entirely with credit cards, and it cost me my sanity, my serenity, my day job, and my well-being. The CD turned out lovely, but it didn't save me financially from anything, didn't hit the big-time, and didn't pay off my debt by a long shot. I was in deep trouble, landed flat on my face, and had to start all over again with nothing, and it was the hardest thing I have ever been through. I didn't save for my CD, or fund it as I was making it. I put the cart before the horse and ran up a ton of debt, and it nearly killed me.

The second time I made a music CD, I saved for it. I opened a CD recording savings account at my credit union and stashed a bit of cash every month for several years. In the meantime, I worked with a technical recording school in the Bay Area, paid an engineer a small amount to help me, and we worked once a month on Sundays, using the studio for free. I paid a couple hundred dollars to each of several musicians for sessions (some of the musicians graciously offered to play gratis), and I worked those amounts into my monthly spending plan or drew from my CD fund. When it came time to mix and master, I had just over $2,200 saved, and I found a terrific professional who did a brilliant job for that amount.

That clarity meant two important things: (1) I had to get comfortable with a slower, steadier timeline, and (2) I had to cover everything I needed with the cash I had. Being clear about what I had to spend helped guide me to the person who could do the best job for what I could pay. And it all worked out swimmingly.

That's what clarity offers us. It offers a chance to fully fund what we love, and to use our ingenuity to get what we need artistically. It's "creativity, not credit cards," as I like to say. And that commitment imparts to us the patience we need to let our gifts unfold at a normal, or even slow, pace. Now that my CD has been released, there is no pressure, no angst, no regret, and nothing but joy surrounding my project. That's the point. It can now go out into the world without any anxiety or difficulty. There are no handprints on its back, desperate for instant outcomes.

That's what I mean when I say we need to fully fund what we love as we're engaging in it. It's the best thing in the world we can do for ourselves as artists, as creators, and for our art itself.

And when our project is complete, we feel nothing in our heart but elation that we showed up, answered the call, funded it, and finished it.

Live On Less for a Cause.

Living within my means opened up the first choices I ever had to live on less for a cause. That cause, for me, was—and is—my art. Absolutely.

Meaning, since I now know what it costs me to live and how to live within the categories I set out for myself each month, I can *voluntarily choose to downsize* those amounts, so I can work my day job less and give more hours to art.

How do I make that work?

It's a very simple addition equation. I downsize my spending in whichever categories are flexible (clothes, dry cleaning, etc.), then downsize bills I don't really need (newspaper subscriptions, cable, etc.), and I live on a simpler plan. And because I have clarity in all my finances, I can know in a few short minutes how much more time I can buy myself by living on less.

For example: Last fall I wanted to write my first play. It had been rumbling around in my head and heart for a few years, and I was ready to get it out on the page. I took a look at my spending plan, talked to my husband to make sure we were covering all we needed to, and then mapped out an amount I could generate to cover my part of Bills, Savings, and Daily Needs. (I knew, from writing my book, what I had to earn to cover the basics, and so I could pull that downsized spending plan out and use it again for reference.)

It had to be enough, realistically, to cover what groceries cost, what fuel costs, what drugstore items cost, etc., in a month's worth of living. It had to have some leeway for things that are unexpected—in other words, savings that I put away in a short-term savings account, including a healthy reserve for emergencies. It had to cover the predictable annual expenses, such as car repairs, vacation, and holiday expenses. But within that framework, I could choose to downsize my expenses *and* my day job-work hours, earning less, but giving myself more art hours.

If that means I'm shopping at the vintage store when I feel like buying clothes, then so be it. If it means I'm buying $5 makeup, then I'll do it. If it means I'm ironing a few more shirts versus sending them out to the dry cleaners, then fire up the iron!

My job is to make art. That's what I do in the world. And sometimes, with the clarity of my spending plan, I choose to live on less for my own clear art cause. Right now, that cause is the book I'm writing for you. Last fall, it was writing my play.

That said, my object isn't to underfund my life indefinitely. That's sort of like going on a never-ending diet. We can do it for a set period of time, but if we deprive ourselves for too long, we end up falling off the diet and rebelling. Financially, that's called underearning, and it's not what we're after. What we are after is the ability to live more simply when we choose to; to live a more basic existence for something we want more than flush daily spending. It's a very powerful choice to be able to make. And our financial clarity allows us to make it.

There's another piece of living simply that we must get comfortable with. While our best friends might be investing in a cabin in the mountains or a Jet Ski for the family, we're going to be funding our art. And we have to make peace with that. Our allotted cash, our extra cash, and our carved-out-as-best-we-can cash is going to need to go toward our creativity. Particularly if we are choosing to live on less in favor of more art time.

And that's fine. We're entitled to that choice. Art is what we love; it's what we long for. So we craft our life around it. We don't apologize or try to keep up with the Joneses. We live humbly, clearly, and with the clarity of no money pressure, so that we can stay engaged in what we're passionate about our whole life long.

That's what this walk is about. It's about putting the supports under our feet that offer us the choices that we really, truly want to make for ourselves. And there is incredible power in those choices.

Know When to Say When.

Artists always ask me, "How do I know when to give up my day job? When is it safe for me to be supported solely by my art?"

This is one of the most important questions an artist can ask herself or himself.

First—and I have to say this—we must get comfortable with the thought that we might have a day job for our whole life. The thing is—and though this is hard to admit to ourselves, it's a truism—we have no control over outcomes, over how our artwork will be received in the marketable world. What that means is that we can't just go roller-coasting out into our daily life with no supports under our feet just because we feel like it. If we want to be an art maker, we have to fund our life.

But don't get me wrong. I believe it's an absolutely worthy and attainable goal to support ourselves with our art, and if it's possible at all in the world—which it is—then it's possible for *us*. That said, making peace with having a day job allows us to work free from angst, and that's what we want to be able to create well: angst-free art hours.

So, I encourage you not to spend time longing for the day when you will no longer need a day job. Just work well, professionalizing your artwork over time, and get comfortable with the gradual pace of moving into a full-time artist's life. Then, when the time comes, you'll be ready.

If you are at a point in your work where you are earning significantly through your art, there are some practical guidelines that can help you know when to say when and leave your day job.

First, we need to generate all of our monthly expense money from our art. In other words, enough to live on and live decently. As we noted before, that means we have to have absolute clarity regarding what it costs us to live each month, and what that bottom-line income number is that keeps us from struggling. On either a downsized plan or a fuller spending plan, we have to cover the stuff that keeps our needs attended to: rent, food, fuel, clothes, savings, car repairs, emergency fund, vacation—all of the things that make for a healthy and balanced life.

For me, I earn about 25 percent of my income from my paintings, music, and writing, and some years it's more or less, depending on what's sold or what's in development. Since that income fluctuates a lot from year to year, I won't be leaving my day job anytime soon. My creative earnings alone are not yet enough to live on in this instance, and since I downsized my spending significantly to be able to teach yoga instead of writing grants, I don't have a lot of room to cut expenses. But since I made the effort to get a day job I love, I'm not anxious about leaving, and my art income can grow at a normal pace over time.

Again, if you can cut expenses significantly to buy yourself more art time and cut hours at a day job, that's great. Go ahead and do it. If you can cover all your needs with your art income, bravo! Then exit your day job gracefully. But you must have *absolute clarity* in your spending so you do not add the worry of money pressure, debt, or poverty to your art life.

Since we usually get paid in larger chunks for artwork when it sells, and not on a monthly or biweekly basis, we have to learn how to make that money last. We can't go out spending our once-every-six-months' art earnings as if we get paid every month like that. We don't get a regular paycheck, so we have to be thoughtful about how we're using our art income, and make it last until the next sale.

For example, if you earn $8,000 or $10,000 of art income when you sell a piece of your work, and you're living on that money, that cash has to last you until you sell the next piece. So, you'll need to parse out how many months of expenses— less your taxes—you can cover on that sale. And since you don't know when you'll sell the next piece, you'll need a reserve to cushion you if you don't sell again within the time-line you expect.

When you first venture out into the art-only money world, and you're not used to living solely on your art income, you'll need some cash to start yourself off. That means, you've got to have some living expense money saved, and some idea of how long you can live on those funds before you need to go back to the day-job world.

My guidelines are these: Have at least six months of liv-ing expenses saved plus some emergency savings and a bit of short-term savings before you consider leaving your day job. When your living expense reserve drops to the level of being able to cover three months of expenses and there's no *confirmed* art sales coming up, go back to work and get another day job. Don't wait. The truth is, even for jobs in restaurants, food stores, small shops, and more, it can take up to three months to get work. Don't drag your feet and don't complain about it. Just do what you need to do to manage your art life well. You don't want to stress yourself out by waiting too long and becoming desperate. That energy will not serve your artistry or your well-being.

So, get and keep a day job until your art is earning at least enough to live on a downsized expense plan—covering your Bills, your Daily Needs, and a little extra for Savings with a little to spare.

When we're thoughtful in our day job movements and keep good, solid art supports under our feet, we can gracefully move into an art-income-supported life without any strain on our heart. And that's what we're after—grace, ease, and a firm foundation for continuing to make art all our life long.

4:

MASTER
YOUR TIME

Do Your Art, No Matter What Else Is Going On.

So, now we've got ourselves a day job, a spending plan, and a willingness to answer our heart's call and show up for art. Now what?

Now, we've got to figure out how to make *time* for our art. We've done the right thing: We've put the supports under our feet to make the art we're longing to make. Now how do we get to it?

Our first step is to find a way to manage and master our time. This is probably the most important thing we will ever learn in relation to our art. So, we're going to get into some genuine detail on this topic. In this chapter and the next, we'll talk about the philosophy of mastering art time and how to position ourselves mentally and emotionally so that we develop work ethics. Then, in the chapter entitled "Map Your Art Life," we'll apply a practical time plan just as we did with our finances.

Remember, none of these ideas about living an artist's life matter unless we have a mechanism for applying them. Talking about them and not having a plan to implement them gets us nowhere. That's what this book is all about—offering simple, practical tools to live healthily and well as an artist. Know that we're going to do more than chat about this. We're going to work on it until we've got it down.

So, let's talk time. Here's the hidden gift in keeping a day job: It's going to impose a schedule on us. I know many of you are crying out, "But that's the problem! I want more time for my art! I don't *want* to spend all those hours at work!" And yeah, I get it. When you have a day job, it eats up a lot of your time. But let's turn this rock over and look at the other side.

You've probably heard the adage, "If you want to get something done, give it to a busy person." That's the skill we're going to employ here to get to our art. We know we have to put supports under our feet in order to create well and ward off poverty and panic. Stress and worry do not make for creative freedom, nor do they contribute to our willingness to keep working. We know that now.

So, we're going to learn to use our busy schedule—that's our art, our day job, and our life—to create days filled with *direction* and *meaning*.

But let's take a moment right now and distinguish the difference between the workaholic, can't-ever-sit-down, manic behavior of what we sometimes mistakenly call "busy," and the efficiency of people who have learned to do what's meaningful first, rather than fill their days with urgent nothingness.

We're not looking to become workaholics who don't know how to rest or vacation, or who never hang it up long enough to go to a movie. That kind of swirling is a behavioral process addiction, and that's not what we're after. We're looking to become the kind of busy people who accomplish much because we're *motivated*. We have *vision* in our heart, and we're driven—in a passionate way, not an addictive way—to make something creative.

We long for our art, and so we make time for it. That's what we're after. This is the approach that leads to a full life: a perspective of feeling blessed to have much we want to do and much we *can* do in the world. We're not bored and we're not boring.

Next, let's tell an awful truth. Would-be artists who don't need day jobs often waste time. When I moved from Los Angeles—where many of my friends were working jobs to support their art—to the affluent San Francisco suburbs, I encountered something I wasn't familiar with. There were whole groups of "early-retired" or supported adult women and men who had had careers of one kind or another, or who had made it big in the tech industry, and who now wanted to make art but could not motivate themselves to work on it. They had enough money to not need a job and were willing to do all kinds of community activism, attend to grown and adult children, or engage in church or temple work, but they couldn't bring themselves to sit down and write or sing or paint or draw. And though community work and activism are good things to do when we have free time, they're not noble when used as a time filler to stuff, bury, and avoid our art.

My point is this: We cannot assume that because we have more time we will automatically use it well. In fact, for many people, the opposite is true. So, until we train ourselves to use our time as best we can—which our day jobs force us to do—we are not ready for the open-ended schedule of no commitments.

We must develop the muscle of good time usage or we will never get anything done. And our day jobs make us face off with our own issues with time.

To put it differently, we need to learn how to be an artist no matter what else is going on. We want to acquire the skill of working over the long term, through time crunches, family pressures, personal challenges, melt-down disasters—through all of it—and still make art. Once we master that, we'll have a work ethic that we will use and hold on to our whole artistic life.

All You Have to Do Is Listen and Act.

We're not usually very good at hearing the first musings of artistic guidance and answering quickly with action. We usually wait too long, hanging back in our insecurity over outcomes, avoiding setting aside the hours needed to explore our calling. When we hesitate and hide out like that, we're essentially editing ourselves and blocking our voice before we even take a step. And it usually ends up making us angry, agitated, depressive, and hard to be with.

So, it's important to know that listening to our own guidance and carving out blocks of hours for ourselves is a skill we can learn. And our day job is going to help us with that by holding our feet to the fire with a schedule. Endless unscheduled time is not being offered to us, so we have to sculpt our art time from a real-world schedule, then honor it and use it.

We also have to learn tools for beginning, for taking action on an idea. We're looking for support that will help us start with nothing, then help us take a first, then a second, and then a third step in our ideas' directions.

There's the Goethe thing: "Whatever you can do or dream you can, begin it. Boldness has genius, power, and magic in it."

But the fact that Goethe himself was from another era—an era when benefactors and rich people and states and churches funded their sons and daughters who wanted to paint or write or sing—can stop us in our tracks. We promote our own time-hesitation by saying, "Our country doesn't fund the arts," or "All artists are poor and struggling and who wants that?" or "No one can make a living as an artist unless they've gone to a major art school and have been handed a stipend or a trust fund."

And art schools, art critics, newspaper arts sections, and art magazines promote this kind of thinking. That somehow in order to be a professional artist—in other words, in order to create with ambition—you must have special privileges in the world of money, time, training, fully-formed talent, and prestige. They train us to think we are less professional if we have to have a day job and have to work hard at managing our time to create an artistic practice. And that's just wrong.

So, as we're learning to set aside time for our artistic calling, or even if we're practiced at it, we have to remember what we said before. That is, that this walk is not about the hype or the hope or the trust fund that someone else has: *It's about the work.* It's not about anything else. It's about listening, as best we can, for the pure, honest, open-hearted song from the musical heart of our own creativity, and then setting aside time to get that melody out into the real world.

It's about hearing, showing up, and acting on what we hear.

Give Up the Privilege Myth.

Let me relieve you of the notion of privilege-as-a-necessity-to-create right now. That's *bunk.* Will it help if you want to be a film director and your mother's a director, too, and she trains you on a set? Maybe. But primogeniture and prestige are not guarantees that you'll be able to get your ideas out of your head, or that you'll learn discipline and discernment, or that you'll ever develop your own sense of composition.

So, what's the privilege myth about, anyway? The privilege mythology is about time. It's a myth about getting there *faster,* and "before" everybody else, with—supposedly—less struggle. So, let's take that apart for a second.

How I can get someplace "before" another artist when my process is uniquely my own? How can I tell when that incredible mix of my life experience that sings to the world—struggles included—is going to play itself out at its fullest? *I can't.*

We think, "Oh, if I just didn't have to have a day job and if my father was a movie executive, I'd be making award-winning films by now." Who says? Marketing people use focus groups and feedback sessions all the time for projects that were geared up for green-lighted, full-budget blockbusters, and still their products fail. So, there's no "knowing" that we'd succeed instantly with a faster, more privileged, and better-funded timeline.

And that's the beauty of our artistic gifts: They're percolating all the time, no matter what's going on in our life—uphill battles included—and they just keep getting richer.

Raymond Carver had only moments late at night to write after grueling day jobs, tense relationships, putting kids to bed, and dealing with his own alcoholism. And he wrote anyway. He wrote on top of the washing machine in the laundry room because that's the only place he could get some privacy. His style—brief, several-page short stories, minimalist and clean—developed because that's all he had time for. And in the process he created a whole new short story genre that revolutionized the fiction world.

So, we just don't know where accomplishment is going to come from. It may be that our own duking it out on the battlefield of life is the very thing that will propel us forward.

The point of giving up the privilege myth is this: Behind every great, materialized idea is an artist who chose to listen for her or his own calling, for a singular voice specific to that call, and then *sat down to work*. At the end of the day, that's all that really matters.

Money, privilege, or being handed the reins of the family business won't do the trick. So, I invite you to check the timeline and privilege prejudices you're holding against your-self at the door.

If your parents weren't professional poets and you didn't get to go to the Iowa Writers' Workshop for two years, who gives a damn? The muse is no respecter of persons. Your heart's experience is as unique as anyone else's on the planet, and if you're called to share it, then—I say—prepare yourself to set aside time, and share it.

It's all on you for one obvious reason: No one else can replicate your artist's voice. *No one.*

Do What's Important First, Not What's Urgent, or "How the Hell Do I Get Started?"

Here's the crux of it: If we're motivated to make art and we still have to go to work, raise a family, care for our aging father, pick up the kids from school, cook dinner, nurture a love relationship, pay the bills, and so on, how in hell do we do it all? How do we carve out time for our creativity when every other obligation seems to tear us away from it?

I'm not sure who said it first, but it's been repeated many, many times: "Stop filling your days with what's urgent. Do what's *important* first."

Urgency is all of the crap that masquerades as import-ant but won't matter 30 seconds after you've done it. What's important is the stuff that's meaningful—not to someone else, but to *you*. It's the stuff that makes you feel you've engaged in who you are, in what you have to offer, and makes you feel good about yourself—from the inside out—when you're done working on it.

A few days ago my husband and I were visiting a friend who is longing to write. Although she allowed herself to leave the country to visit her extended family for a good, long visit, she refuses to give herself the present of a writing class once a week, "because my teenage kids need me." It's doubtful that her family life will fall apart if she takes a three-hour class once a week—and it certainly didn't when she was overseas away from her kids for a whole month. But that's the mentality many of us have. We refuse to give ourselves what we need to support our art, and then we're less satisfied with our life. It's a bad, bad equation—a sum of overbusyness, urgency, and resentment that breeds an internal unhappiness and a brooding lack of fulfillment.

So, prepare yourself now to set aside time to do your art. Even if you don't know how you're going to do it or what you're going to do, ready yourself to spend time on it.

That's what artists do: We spend time on our art.

We've All Got 24 Hours, so Start Strategizing Your Time.

I remember having a hand-waving argument with my husband once when he shouted, "When do *I* get time to write?" And I yelled back, "If you want to write, that's between you and your God! We've all got 24 hours!" We both stood there for a moment frozen and stunned with the truth of it: Both of us had issues with setting aside time to do our art. Both of us had resistance to sitting down, or what writers often call "beating the room."

Beating the room means overcoming the distractions of all of the stupid, urgent stuff that calls out to us when it's time to do our art, stuff that *pretends* to be pressing, and that stands in the way of doing real, honest, creative work.

After the "you-and-your-God" moment, we both changed our approaches to time. Saturdays from 9 a.m. to 2 p.m. became his sacred writing time. We didn't make plans. I didn't interrupt. That was his art time.

When I worked on my art, I painted by the clock, two hours each session. I wrote an entire book by writing one hour a day, four days a week, by the timer. If I missed an hour one day, I owed myself the hour the next day. It took a year and eight months to write my book—a while, but not that long. And what else was I doing that was so excruciatingly important that I couldn't set aside four hours a week to work? *Nothing.*

There was, as I found out, nothing stopping me but myself.

Get Practical and Get Real.

Here's the thing about time: We've got to make it work for us by being practical. We can't hang out in the world of *dabbling* and expect to develop the chops necessary to get our art out in the world in a professional and meaningful way.

Dabbling—or not showing up for ourselves on a regular basis—translates into a messy, emotional mudslide down our creative peak. It won't produce good work, and instead, cooks up voluminous amounts of self-doubt, self-hatred, and self-flagellation.

So, we have to get *concrete* about managing our time—especially since we've got obligations, day jobs, and a life to manage, too.

How do we do this?

First, we get practiced at setting aside *reasonable amounts of time* to do our art. And we won't know what's truly reasonable until we get in there and muck around with our weekly hours for a bit. That means we have to practice using our hours the way we *think* they might work, and keep adjusting them until they actually *do*.

Don't expect that you're going to get this right out of the gate. You're going to have to explore, try, fail, and retry until you get it right for yourself.

Can you reasonably write one hour a day, several days a week, and keep your head in your piece? Do you need at least a two-hour window in your art studio to set up, work, clean up, and get something meaningful done? Can you work on composing songs in half-hour blocks or do you need more time?

I've figured out that when I'm writing nonfiction, I need at least one hour a day, four or five days a week, working by the clock. Nonfiction lives in my head like a puzzle, and I resist it more than writing fiction, so I need the structure of an imposed timeline. With fiction—writing a play or a short story—I enjoy it so much that I can just give myself over and offer it every free moment I've got until it's done. With painting I need short warm-ups when I haven't been at the easel for a while—that is, midsize paper pieces I can knock out easily before I take on a huge, several-hour-per-session abstract canvas.

But I didn't learn any of this until I got in there and got my hands dirty. And just because my time theory works for now doesn't mean it will work forever. It has changed many times and it will surely change again.

The crux of it is this: If one time approach doesn't work to motivate me, then I have to try something else. That's the adult land of time management. I have to be responsible to my artistic gifts, keep working my schedule, and keep showing up for my art until I've got a groove going that keeps me working steadily.

I keep near at hand something I call my "Unsurpassed Time-Guidance List." These are the principles I go back to again and again when I'm struggling with sitting down to do my art, and they're what we will refer to in the next chapter when we craft our artist's Time Map. Here they are:

- Set aside a reasonable chunk of time and calendar it.
- Don't make ANY other plans.
- Don't answer the phone. Turn all nearby phones

OFF at least 10 minutes before you're scheduled to begin.

- Don't text, don't open e-mail, don't use the computer for any use other than for art (e.g., if you write).
- Turn off all alarms and noise notifications on all devices.
- Don't do "this one little thing." Just sit down.
- Underwhelm yourself: Think of what you want to get done in the chunk of time you have, then cut it by two-thirds.
- Give yourself breathing room: Take slow, steady steps.
- Don't rush.
- Trust that there will be more time later on— tomorrow, the next day, or next week.
- Remember that slow, regular work hours get much more accomplished than big bursts.
- Remind yourself that everything takes three times longer than you expect.
- Work at a normal pace.
- Get rid of outcome expectations: Work for the joy of having your hands in your art.
- Feel good about every hour you put in.

One last little thing about time. Don't think that if you keep pushing harder and harder, it will make you succeed faster or earn more. Trust the process. Live and work and share your art at a normal, healthy pace. Work steadily and do what you need to do to keep your spirits up, your head in, and your being strong.

Show Up for Your Art Hours as if It's a Job.

If there's one piece of advice I can offer that can change your life regarding your art, it is this: Show up for your scheduled art hours as if it's a job. Take it that seriously.

When you do, the whole world shifts beneath your feet. You feel better about yourself. You become less attached to outcomes. You show up willing and ready, and your work begins to flow, unobstructed, and full of your gifts.

I have a friend who gets a gift of $2,000 to $3,000 each year from her parents. She puts it in a savings account and then uses it to pay herself when she does her artwork. She gives herself $10 an hour, adds to the account a bit each month, and pays herself for her art hours for a good part of the year. It's a terrific idea, professionalizing her work, and it gets her to show up each week and really dig in. I have another friend who writes children's books and works for a Trader Joe's grocery store, and on each 15-minute break, he sets his timer, sits down and writes, and puts a groovy little sticker on his notebook page when he's done writing to acknowledge his work.

The point is to use whatever you can get your hands on to help you show up for your appointed art hours. Pay yourself. Make yourself accountable to a friend. Create a gold-star chart for yourself. Keep a diary or a "gratefulness journal" where you chart your hours and give yourself credit. Or keep it really simple and take a moment after every art session to say "thank you" to yourself. Be willing to be that honorable about your hours and see how your work opens up and grows.

Remember: Start simply. Do not spend so much time the first day that you don't want to spend any the following day. Start, but start small. (We'll talk about how to apply this guidance practically in the next sections.)

Honor your code with yourself, which is to listen, take steps, and keep working.

We're in this for a Lifetime.

Once we surrender to the fact that we're artists, we will realize something about time that's particularly profound. That is, we're in this for a lifetime.

We're not going to retire from our artistic soul when we're 65. We're going to hear our callings all of our days—meaning, once we're in, we're in for the long haul.

That means we have to develop strategies, approaches, outlooks, and time habits that are going to support us over a number of years, and over many cycles of work, styles, and transition times.

Long after Picasso's huge success story, he kept working—making hundreds and hundreds of line drawings, inventing a new art form for himself. Who cares that his middle-years stuff is more celebrated now? Who knows what will be celebrated a century from now? The thing is, he had a work ethic, and he kept working because his heart was in the art, not the outcomes.

I remember when I first recognized how different my time-path would be as an artist from other people's. I was driving by a tennis court on my way to acting class after a full day of work at my day job, and I looked over at the people on the court and thought, "I won't be playing tennis on Thursday nights, will I?" And I was sad for a while after that, realizing I would always have multiple "jobs" with my art: my day job, and the work of expressing multiple creative gifts.

I realized I would always have ideas that were building up in me, and things that I wanted to explore artistically, and the force of that was always going to be there, pressing down on me, time-wise. Long hours of leisure time weren't going to be a part of my world. And it gave me pause, for sure.

But I also recognized something else: *I was never going to be bored.* I would always have what I needed to live an engaged life, one that I value and am proud of. And when I'm 89, I'll still have things I want to say and create. I'll still be *in.*

And that's what we should want as artists: to be fully alive the whole time and to leave everything we've got on the field, no yard line left uncovered, no goal line left unexplored.

Our heart, our soul, our willingness, and our time—it's all going to get offered on the altar of our artistry.

5:
GROW SOME
WORK ETHICS

Don't Wait for Inspiration; Just Work.

Inspiration, by itself, is as fickle as a Hollywood boyfriend with a monogamy issue. First it flits around your head, dazzling you with its light, and then kisses you full on, right on the mouth as it vaporizes, leaving no trace of having ever been near you.

On its own, inspiration is not reliable—not by a long shot. It's often late, absent, missing in action, or otherwise belligerently withholding when we most want it to show up.

The good news is, we don't need it to work. Inspiration, as it turns out, is already there inside us without us having to wait for it or work on acquiring it. It is our own voice, inseparable from our own self, and it is wrapped inside the call to create. What we need is a vehicle for listening to it, a work ethic for getting what we've heard *out*. Showing up to work provides that opening.

Somerset Maugham once said, "I write when inspiration strikes; *fortunately, it strikes every morning at nine a.m. sharp.*"

That's the upshot. The divine spark of our own unique voice respects us when we sit down to work. Many, many times as artists we will have to start working before the spark shows itself in full form. When we do this over and over again—sitting down to work at our appointed time—inspiration will be there, too, banging down the door to get in on the action.

As artists we have to learn to trust. But what the hell does that really mean, in practical terms? It means we have to trust the ground as it shifts beneath us and changes shape. We have to have faith when the laying down of our work is coming out in the spurts and distorted shapes of early efforts. We need to train ourselves to know that it's always like that at first: cold and dark in the predawn morning, with our feet freezing and our eyes tearing, long before the sun comes up and makes it clear that the light will, indeed, find us.

We have to be willing to start with nothing and just work.

Inspiration respects us when we're brave, when we take a chance, and when we make the effort to bring our expressions into shape and form. We can trust that when we do, the strength of our idea-to-form muscles will build and grow and make us strong as oxen.

"Start Here": Get Some Tools to Help You.

What practical tools can we use to help us get our ideas out of our head? Beyond our talent and our willingness to sit down and work, what skills do we need to develop to create and keep creating?

First, we need some tools to help us get started or get back in when we've been away from our art for hours or days.

A teacher I once worked with gave me a terrific tool for sorting out what to do next (or first) called "The Walking Meditation." The Walking Meditation is for those days when I can't sit still, can't concentrate, and can't focus long enough to get my idea out of my head. It's a procrastination-ender, making me responsible to my work by using my walking time to sort out where I'm going artistically.

Here's what I do. I go outside and do a little meditation that goes something like this: "I'm dedicating this half-hour of walking to figuring out where I want this canvas to go, and what I'm trying to get across." Or, "I'm using this next hour to help me focus on which project wants to come next." And then I walk. It works with anything creative or anything I'm struggling with or need to find direction on.

Another amazing way to jump-start our work—particularly if we're beginning something new or have just finished a project—is to ask ourselves, *What would thrill my heart? What do I want next for myself and my art?*

Then, once we have even a vague notion of what's meaningful to us, we get a schedule. As I've said before, setting aside concrete hours to work is where the rubber meets the road, where the actual birthing of something can come into being.

Do you need at least two consecutive hours to sculpt your abstract nude? Can you get meaningful work done on your East Indian travel memoir on weekly Saturday mornings? Does one afternoon a week of your brass-and-gold jewelry-making make you want to waste time and three one-hour sessions don't? Do you need at least two months of exploring on a giant canvas before you'll be able to tell if the format works for you?

We need simple, easy, practical tools, such as schedules and meditations, because the creative act is unlike anything else we do in our American linear timeline. When we're writing a book on a subject on which we have no historical expertise, or starting a gallery when we've never run one before, or beginning to paint abstracts just because we find them fascinating, we are going to need support. We are going to need tools to help us listen for which way to go. No doubt, some days we will need to grab on to anything that floats to get us across the moat of self-doubt and sheer terror.

That said, I'm not a believer in spending hours and hours with prep tools. There's tons of artist advice out there about journaling and meditating for hours, cleaning and setting up your workspace—even doing your sewing when you're blocked—and it's all advice for people who don't have day jobs. Our time is precious, and so our prep tools need to be short and sweet. No two-hour journaling sessions that steal our actual art time.

So, take some time and sort out what will help get you started and keep you engaged, but know that soul satisfaction is in the work, not in the ramp-up. Classes (where you have to show up), deadlines (to someone who will hold you accountable), and schedules are all good places to begin. An artist without practical tools tends to get lost and give up. Don't do that. Just adopt what helps you work.

I have a sign in my studio that says "Start Here." What

that means is, *just begin*. Start with a blank canvas and begin to apply paint. Start with nothing and *work*. There will be no paint-by-numbers, written outline for anything I want to do, say, or express, so I just have to start the train rolling and begin any way I can.

I guess. I try. I improvise. I intuit. And I work.

As Sam Shepard said, quoted by Patti Smith in her book *Just Kids*, "You can't [screw it up.] It's like drumming. If you miss a beat, you create another."

That's what we do. We step in, with courage, use our tools, and begin.

How Do You Know What to Work on First?

What if we have multiple interests or many "callings"? Most artists have "crossover": If they can paint, they may also be able to sing torch songs, or costume design, or bake gourmet cakes, or forge metal sculptures, or do some other form of creative work that may "call" them in the professional sense.

If we don't know which call to answer, or if we're working on listening to the chatter in our heart over what's eating at us creatively to move on something, how do we know which first step is a go?

I have two approaches to this artists' challenge and both are simple. One is to answer the loudest call first. If your heart has been at you for five years to take guitar lessons, then start there.

In the first few months of learning 10 or 12 chords and

getting some fingering down on the guitar, I wrote a song a week. It was like someone turned on a switch in me and out they came. Not all of them were good, mind you, but some of them were. My artistic self had been pressing on me for years, just waiting for me to open the door, and once I did, all of that stored musical poetry came flowing out onto the page.

The press of the thing you're most pregnant with may not end up being what you'll end up with. But I have found that it is the best starting point, and it will lead you down the path of artistic growth, toward something that you may not be able to see yet, but will surely be meaningful to you. And that's what you're crafting time for.

The second approach is to set up your life like school. Remember when you had hour-long periods for a bunch of different subjects? Try thinking of your life like that. A few hours a week for exercise, a handful of hours for your day job, two nights a week for pottery class, a Saturday morning for a music jam, Friday date night, Sundays for the family, an hour or two on Sunday night writing poetry.

This is a terrific approach if we're just discovering our artistic talents and just beginning to give them voice. Setting aside time gives us room to see what we have to say. And many times we surprise ourselves.

For instance, when I sat down to write my debt-free living book, I had no historical expertise in finance, I had no "authority" other than my own fall-on-my-face financial disaster and subsequent debt-recovery experience, and I had no burning desire to write about debt. What I had was a push from friends who kept saying, "Hey, this works—you should share this," or "This saved my marriage—you really need to write this down." And by carving out some time and giving myself over to the exploration of it, I realized I had quite a bit to say that had not been said before. And a whole book came out of that opening, a book that helped a lot of people and made me feel great about the helping.

The point is, we want to be able to develop the discipline to sit down and try things so we get what's rambling around in our artist's head and heart *out*, and work on it long enough to decide whether those things are compelling enough to continue on to a finish line. But we'll never know if we don't give ourselves room to take a concrete look.

Finally, if your job allows you to have flexible hours, or you can live well on a part-time gig, then use your time well. *Don't waste it.* Write out a schedule that gives you a few hours in each area where you have gifts and show up to work with integrity and ethics. (We will talk about the practical application of art schedules in the next chapter.)

Beat the Room.

We all know about procrastination. Every artist on earth knows how hard it is to "beat the room," or to beat back the minutiae of pressing but meaningless crap that invades our minds the minute we attempt to sit down and do our art.

Suddenly, the dish drainer in the kitchen just *has* to get emptied and the floor needs scrubbing. Suddenly, that box in the car that we forgot to bring inside just *has* to get moved into the house and its contents stuffed onto closet shelves. Suddenly—and creepily, since it eats up whole hours like that retro Japanese film *The Blob*—17 e-mails that suck up two hours just *have* to get answered. And—poof!—there goes our art time.

I don't even have to go into the details of how we get swirling with the meaningless stuff that wastes our time: We all know the pull of the nonimportant and the hangover of guilt and shame it leaves in its wake.

So, how do we combat the urge to bleed away our time from what's most important to us?

First, we have to let ourselves off the hook for having the sensations that make us want to waste time in the first place. Wasting time—or filling it with things that are faux-important, such as e-mail—is a fear defense mechanism. Simply put, we're afraid that what we're about to do won't be good enough, won't sell, or won't turn out the way we want it to. And that means we're caught up in outcomes and not in the artistic process.

When we catch ourselves doing that—swirling in procrastination, fearful of outcomes—we can coach ourselves down off the wall with four simple words. They are: *It's about the work.* It's not about the outcomes. What's going to make us feel better, what's going to build our self-esteem, is to *do* the work. That's all. Just sit down and do it, no matter how it turns out.

Then we have to identify "circling behavior." That is,

the hovering around our workspace, doing little things like cleaning or arranging our painting rags, or reorganizing our woodcarving tools in their bins. This isn't work, either. This is using our time to "helicopter" our work: buzzing around it but not really doing it.

When I catch myself procrastinating, circling, or helicoptering, I apply the visual of a giant stop sign in my mind. I say out loud, "Stop! It's about the *work*. It's about doing what's important first, not what's urgent."

Doing what's important first is the key to all great art. The urgent stuff we do all week long will be unmemorable the moment we're done with it. We will not care about it *at all* in one year, two years, ten years. But we will care—and care deeply—when we look back with pride on the art we created five years ago, and we will feel proud and brave that we had the courage to beat the room and make something that touches us, and touches others. That's *important*.

All the rest of it can take a friggin' backseat and sit there until we're damn well done with our art. That's discipline. That's courage. And that's what will live on in our heart as lasting, meaningful, and soul-fulfilling.

Support Your Artist's Work Ethic with a Schedule and a Timer.

Napoleon Hill said it best: "A goal is a dream with a deadline." In other words, the most powerful thing you can do as an artist is to make time commitments to yourself and keep them.

The discovery that changed my artist's life was learning how to work by the timer. My weekly schedule helps me map my time, but it's the timer that makes sure I honor my hours, even when I don't feel like working. (All I have to do is look at the *rest* of my week to remember that my art time is precious.)

And even though I often keep a little handwritten version of my schedule in my bag so I can't go vague on myself, ending up at the discount store looking for bedsheets instead of doing my art, I still need the timer to hold myself accountable to my *actual* work hours, the ones I know will make me feel like I've done what I set out to do.

What the timer also offers, besides working deadlines, is time to *explore*. We often don't know what we're going to write or collage or compose when we begin, or even when we're in the middle. So, we need a tool to help us give ourselves permission to sit there and craft it out—to work it like a puzzle and take the time to pore over ideas, then hammer them into place and build the thing, block by block.

And it's not just beginning a piece that can stump us and stall us. Sometimes we're in the middle when we most need the support of a timer: the portion where we're getting *some* traction, but the full form or theme hasn't shown itself to us yet, and the construction of it is testing our imagination and our skill.

Completing a work can be even harder. Our resistance

often shows its ugly head right when we're on the verge of actually finishing something, when we know it's almost time to take it out into the professional arena to see if it floats.

All of these humps in our creative journey require us to rev up some kind of inner velocity to get over them. An inexpensive timer is a brilliant little creative operating tool for doing just that.

Whatever you use, make yourself accountable to the time you set aside for yourself and your art. That's the point.

When It All Goes to Hell.

So, what happens when it all goes to hell? Let's say I've got a commitment to write two hours a day, three days a week, and then my husband comes home and needs me to help him load up the table we're refinishing—*right now*—because some guy will give us a half-price deal if we haul it over this very afternoon.

Or let's say your kid calls from school and has a bloody nose and she's hyperventilating and you've got to run her over to the urgent care doctor. Or your refrigerator went kaput, the freezer ice is melting, and there's water all over the floor.

When the whole time thing tanks on us, we remember what we said before: *We need to learn how to work no matter what else is going on.* That doesn't mean we don't stop and do what needs to be done in the moment. We do. But we owe ourselves those two hours *this week.* No bullshit. If we have to get up at 5 a.m. or stay up until midnight to get it done, then that's what we do. We put in our hours.

I know, I know. You're thinking that this is really hardcore—that it's too tough to manage. But think of it this way: Life's unexpected disasters will always show up to cheat us out of our art hours. That's the way a busy life is. And when we beat back the guilt, remorse, anger, and self-loathing that being robbed of our art hours leaves in its wake with a commitment to *work anyway*, we finish the week feeling great about ourselves. We build self-worth and ease every time we show up and honor our art time, and do it no matter what else is going on.

What we're courting here is professionalism. We're after *mastery* with our work ethics. More than the outcomes of our art sessions, more than what we've actually created, we want to know that we can count on ourselves to show up professionally, hour after hour, taking ourselves as seriously as if someone is paying us to do the work.

That's the life of a working artist.

Show Up Until Showing Up Becomes Second Nature.

Art is a practice. And just like practicing yoga or marathon running, learning to love well or being a good parent, it's not an overnight thing. It takes stepping into the stream time and time again, until we come to know the stream as one of our own limbs, as our heart beating automatically in our chest. In other words, we want to learn to show up and show up until showing up becomes second nature.

I like to think of this spiritually—that the Divine is calling me, asking something of me, and I want to have a practice of showing up as fast as possible.

I once said to a favorite clergyman of mine, "I am so sick of learning by pain I could just throw up; it absolutely sucks." And he said, "Well, stop doing that! Learn by grace and intuition." I had no idea what he was talking about. He smiled at me. "Listen closely and act on guidance quickly—that's what I mean. *Obey.* You're being called and you won't move until you hit the wall. Stop that!"

I had never seen myself in that light before: That I was getting messages about what to do all the time, but I had to bang into something and hurt myself before I was willing to move or change.

We don't want to do that. We want to listen and act on our guidance willingly and as quickly as humanly possible. By showing up for ourselves and being responsive to our own guidance we learn the course of our own creative thrust. We learn what works for us. We're surprised, certainly, from time to time, but we know our own arc, our process, our heart, and where we stand on the bedrock of the gifts we're standing up for. We come to know how the Divine speaks to us, how the spark works in us, and how to get it out.

And that, after it's all said and done, is what we're after for our art and for our life.

Work without Regard for Outcomes.

When I was acting, I had many friends who indulged in what I called the "Audition Crazies." They'd whip themselves into a frenzy before a casting call about their chances of getting a role, and then right afterward, get back in the car and start an obsessive chant of "Did I get it? Did I get it? Do you think I got it?" The obsession would command many days while they waited to hear, going over each and every tiny aspect of a five-minute audition with anyone who would listen.

It was outcomes-focused artistry, and it didn't work. The emotional cycles of the high-highs ("I think I got it! I'm sure they liked me!") and the low-lows ("They hate me. I'll never get a job...") were just too much to stomach. For them, and for everyone around them, too.

I learned a lifelong lesson from that experience which changed me forever as an artist. *I learned how to put my work out into the world without losing my mind.* And the key is this: I had to give myself permission to commit to the best work I can do in any moment without regard for the results. In other words, I had to sweat and toil and labor over it, and then bring it out into the world and let it go.

I had to view it like raising a child. I must love and train and respect my child (my art), but when it's time for my kid to move out into the world, I have to let it. I have to give it the opportunity to stand on its own two feet, to cry with it when it falls down, and to cheer for it when it sings and soars and moves people. But I don't own it. Once I birth it and raise it, it's not mine anymore. I have to step back and let it live.

Practice Detachment.

My job is to be a channel for my art, to get it out. But I have to practice some detachment from it once it's "out there" or I will completely lose my sanity. In other words, as we said in the previous section, once I've created my art, worked on it, and sent it out into the world, I have to let it go.

There's the Aristotle thought: "Where my talents and the needs of the world collide, there lies my vocation." And though that seems like it's a straightforward thought, what's most important about that adage is what's unsaid in the sentence. That is, we cannot know how the world will receive our work, and it is codependent nonsense to try to mechanically figure it out or control outcomes. And, should we try to, we will make ourselves crazy trying.

"The needs of the world" are unpredictable, fickle, and even childish sometimes, and success, as we know it, can be vaporous, unworthy, and random. So, we can't put stock in that.

What we can do is put our heart and soul into what we do, and take a loving pride in being courageous enough to do our art in the first place, and then bring the things we work on to completion and out into the light.

I like to look at it this way: I live committed to a particular result in my life—that is, expressing art and being an artist—without being attached to any single, specific outcome or any one individual piece. That way, I get to work with the freedom of staying inside my own discovery process for a lifetime. I can't be governed by what I think other people will want or like. I have to be able to see what I see, for myself, and translate that into my art.

I used to have a Buddhist teacher who said, "We have everything we need inside us to be happy and at peace." What that means to me is this: I have control over nothing in the world of outcomes. What I can manage is how I relate to my work and myself. I can train myself to feel blessed that I get to play in the pool of art *at all* and be happy that I won't arrive at the end of my days wondering what the hell I've done with my life. I get to feel good about who I am in the world based on what I do. I get to be a part of creating.

No matter what the outcome of a piece of work, I get to say that I have courage, I have strength, I am willing, I show up, and I live in the world of artistry. That is how we stay sane and continue to love the arc of our art throughout an entire lifetime.

Know When to Set It on the Shelf.

I once wrote a beautiful cookbook that almost made it to the top at a major publishing house. It was ready to go. Everyone in every department had signed off on it and had said yes. It had a great theme, terrific content, beautiful sample art. And then the company got a new top guy and he said no. Nothing I tried afterward could get it sold. I tried two new agents, every marketing tactic I could come up with, and finally I just had to open my eyes and see the writing on the wall: It wasn't going to happen. It's still on a shelf.

It could be, today, an e-book or a self-published piece if I wanted to make the effort. But I have moved on. What I know about it is it has become fertilizer for my next works. It gave me confidence in my writing ability, my sense of composition, my themes, my talent, and my delivery. It was not, in the least, wasted.

Obviously, in this market, we have new and endless options for self-publishing and self-promotion. And that's a great thing for the novel that no one picked up, the cookbook that no publishing house bought, or the 5-by-8-foot canvas rolled up in the corner of the studio. There are website galleries, self-publishing options, music publishing sites, craft art sites, video and short story galleries, and much, much more. And there are endless numbers of social media promotion avenues.

But don't be fooled: Spending all day trying to create some buzz around a project that's not lifting off the ground is not artwork. It's marketing. And though most of us artists have a hard time finding the willingness to do our marketing work at all (and need encouragement to do so), just remember that we have to balance our time between actual artwork and promotion. Driving ourselves crazy tweeting 20 times a day is not going to keep us sane and fulfilled. Doing our artwork is.

So, when our work isn't reaching people—even after we've taken it out into cyberspace and have done our due diligence with it—it's probably time to set it on the shelf. That means we need to be brave enough to see the writing on the wall, to witness the arc of what's not happening, and move on to the next thing.

Here's how I measure this. When I've given my best and done what's humanly possible without killing myself and nothing is happening, it's usually time to set the thing aside and start the next project.

Let it be fertilizer. Let it fund the next piece with the skills learned. The thing about us artists is that we are lightning rods for creative ideas. All we have to do is listen for them. So, if one isn't landing on people's hearts, no big deal. Call it a success for having completed it, give yourself credit, and move on to the next one.

There'll Be Days Like This.

Yes, we've got to employ supports, and, yes, we've got to experiment with and develop discipline—our own flavor of it—and we've got to use tools like timers and schedules and "get started" exercises. We've got to be committed and we must learn how to use everything in our skills box to become a healthy artist. All of that is true.

But some days it's all going to go to hell in a handbasket and we're going to be emotionally laid out and just plain *bummed*.

The trigger point might be something as simple as hearing that our best friend's rent just went up by $800 a month, then recognizing the fragility of the supports under our feet. Or it could be our old pal from high school calling up to say she just hit the $200,000 mark in her IRA. Or it could be the endless gatekeepers at the door of every one of our artistic efforts, the endless submitting, waiting, and hoping. Just yesterday I read a little quip about a woman who said she felt she "had finally arrived," and it nearly sent me under the bed.

So, it's not always going to be sweeping through the wheat fields with a cape over our shoulders, our hair, and our artist identity cascading in the wind. Being an artist is hard. And it's hard for the very reasons that it is amazing.

It's *separate* from what most other people are doing. Meaning, it's often solitary, in practice as well as in lifestyle. It requires seeing beyond the square-peg, status-quo, office life and envisioning something else, while meanwhile, all the rest of the world beats its drum of monetary success and climb-the-ladder business prowess.

And some days it's just going to knock us over to be walking such a contrary path, and we'll get depressed and hurt, and we'll feel like we're left out—outside of our time and our culture and even our friendship circles.

So, it may be that when your best friends call to say that they've just closed on the beautiful $1.2 million house in the suburbs and you're just keeping it together with your day job and your 700-square-foot apartment, your confidence gets dinged.

And these are the days when we have to take time out to be gentle with ourselves.

It might mean taking an afternoon off and getting outdoors in nature; going for a hike on a mountain trail or a bike ride through a pretty neighborhood. It might mean sitting in the park and playing your guitar for no reason at all except that the sun is shining. It might mean holing up in a comfy chair at the library or a café and sitting there for three hours reading your favorite novel.

When we occasionally fall prey to these kinds of depressive feelings about our artist's life, the most important thing to do is to *stop*. Don't keep pushing when you're tender. Take an hour or two and do something sweet for yourself, something that doesn't cost much and that connects you to an easy feeling of being grateful to be alive.

Dismiss this advice at your own peril. When we're fragile, we need care. As hokey as it might seem, we need extra hugs from our friends and loved ones. We need confidence builders in the form of people we trust letting us know how brave they think we are for living a creative life. We need to talk to other artists about how it feels to walk this path and stay true to our calling.

So, when the day hits that you're knocked under the bed with sadness that it hasn't turned out differently so far, stop and breathe, and take care of yourself. Be gentle, be sweet to yourself, and don't press. Think: Easy on the soul.

And then, remember that no one person's life is of any more value than any other's. We all contribute to our world, and every good thing we offer is meaningful to the whole.

We hold close to our hearts the shining truth that being called as an artist is a blessing rare and exquisite, unreplicated in any other being on the planet.

Take a Break.

When we're multi-talented, balancing a day job-life with an artist's path, we can have the sense that we never get a break from ourselves, and it can feel like those pressure cooker semesters at college when we took too many units and couldn't keep up with the endless reading, pop quizzes, and term papers. When we get obsessed with that "always more to do" feeling, the pressure will surely get to us, and it can completely deplete and drain our spirits.

So, we have to work some relaxation in—do our best to make sure we get some rest and have some fun along the way. Yes, we artists have an extra responsibility in our life that ends up taking precedence over recreational activities. But that doesn't mean we can never take a swimming class or join a cycling team, grow orchids or go skiing. It *does* mean those things won't come first.

The importance of slow, steady steps comes into play right here. We need to be able to have a *life* while we're creating. We need to take regular breaks. We need to take vacations. We have to take time off from all of it sometimes—a week or two or maybe four—to put a break between one project and the next. That's why a day job is so important just now. It supports us not only while we're creating, but while we're resting, too.

Our artist's path will move up and down, and in and out. It is not linear. It will require our passionate, undivided attention at times, and our quiet, meditative exploration at others. It's an inside job, and so we have to take care of our insides as well as our outsides.

Our most pressing objective is to be able to do our art all our life without losing our sanity, our shirt, or our creative way in the process. Without doubt, our artwork will need to change and grow, and we need to have the underpinnings in both habits and character to help it go where it needs to go—including knowing how and when to rest.

Living our art with an ethic of balance—even if we can't see it just yet—is going to bring to us that most elusive of all life qualities: that is, *joy.* And when we walk a balanced path of creativity, love, family, day job, and self-care—in full-on engagement—we will come to know that, with a little practice, fulfillment is ours for the having.

6:

MAP YOUR
ART LIFE

Pin Your Points.

Years ago, my friend Sam Woodhouse shared an exercise he used with his staff as artistic director of the San Diego Repertory Theatre. It's called "Cultural Mapping." He attached a huge world map to the wall, and asked each person to pin the places their family was from, including any place they had lived during their life. Next he asked them to pin the places their parents, grandparents, and great-grandparents had come from. Each person attached their name to the pins, and then he wrapped brightly colored string from pin to pin. The object was for everyone else in the room to get a picture of each person's history and experience, and to evoke empathy, understanding, and inclusion of each person's gifts and viewpoints.

We're going to do a similar thing for our art life, only we will be the beneficiary of our acquired knowledge. This will be our first step in mapping our art life.

This is a simple exercise that's not designed to take up huge amounts of time. As I said before, I don't believe in spending hours in ramp-up exercises when our art time is precious and limited. So, keep it simple.

You can do this exercise on a big blank sheet of butcher paper, some pieced together 8 1/2 by 11 sheets, a single notebook page, or on any surface you choose. It doesn't matter. I like to use a big piece of paper so I can really fill in the margins with little images and notes. You're going to hang this paper up someplace where you can see it, so make the size work with your home space.

Set aside about a half-hour. First, draw a figure in the middle—that's you, and it can be as simple as a stick figure for this exercise—taking up the midline of the page. Then, around this representation of your body, close in, start noting the images that represent the things you love to do. If it's painting, draw a paintbrush. If it's writing, draw a pen or a book or a keyboard. If it's sculpting, draw a hunk of clay or metal or wood. Draw everything you love, surrounding the close circle around your body.

The drawing of our objects is important here, even if we think we can't draw. This isn't a word list; it's an image exercise. We want to be able to look viscerally and quickly at our images and see what's important to us.

My objects are paintbrushes and canvasses, pens and plays and books for writing, guitar for composing, microphone for singing, pans for cooking, a yoga mat for teaching, a closet full of great clothes for pleasure, high heels for going out with my husband, a suitcase for traveling, a sunhat for lying in the sun, a novel for relaxing, a bike for cycling, a martini glass for dining out, a ticket for seeing movies with my film-and-writing-professor husband, and a wedding ring for being happily married.

You can feel free to adorn your "body" with any one of the things you love or do well.

Then in the outer circle draw the things that represent your responsibilities, those you willingly take on for those you love and those that are duties. Anything that takes time can be included here.

Mine are a car for driving to and from yoga teaching, a grocery bag for food and household shopping, a dishtowel and a hammer for work around the house, a cake for visiting with family, a decorative bowl for the many times I cook something for friends who we're socializing with or who are sick, a telephone for reaching out to friends and marketing my artwork, a computer for administrative work, an envelope for the piles of e-mails I answer, a couple of armchairs for visiting with my 94-year-old mother-in-law, a mailing box for submitting my writing and music work, an iPad for studying and making yoga videos.

Feel free to leave the page lying on the table for a few days and come back and add things that occur to you. Once you've drawn in all your images, we'll use them to start helping you prioritize.

This exercise won't lead to a regular pie-chart division of how we're spending our time. Just like the money spending plan idea, what we're looking to establish is a time *plan*—not a record of how we spent our time. Recording how we spend our time after we've spent it is too late. We're looking to *plan* how we spend our hours, based on our true desires and genuine needs. We're looking to banish the stuff that's meaningless and get to the things that are meaningful faster. For now, all we want to do is look at what we say is important to us—the things we drew close to our body—and then, in the outer circle, look at our obligations.

Once your images are complete, tape your sheet up someplace where you can see it for a week or two and just let it sink in. I like to put mine up on my hall closet mirror so I look at it every day.

Here's a quick example of how this helps. When I did this exercise, it became really clear to me that I was spending hours and hours of time driving to meet with acquaintances, socializing with people I hardly knew. I'm friendly, and when I would meet people, I often ended up making plans to get together with them. But these encounters were not deepening into friendships and tended to be transitory—in other words, when measured against my true desires and true responsibilities, I was wasting time. And by looking at my art life map, I could see that those encounters were making me feel pressed for time in my relationship, in my art, and in my work. They were burning up hours—particularly frustrating hours in traffic—that I could use much better elsewhere in my life. With those clear visuals to guide me, I could take some steps to adjust my behavior and put some more balance in my days.

That kind of simple time insight is the first objective of the art map.

Map Your Art Life.

The next step in your mapping exercise is to create an actual Time Map of your daily life. Once we know what our loves, priorities, and duties are, we can start to craft a schedule based on our needs and desires. Know that every single person's art map is going to be different. Meaning, though I'm going to offer practical ways to do this, ultimately you're going to be the one who determines how to make this work.

Just like the money spending plan, I'm not going to tell you what should be important to you or what you should include in your Time Map. It's not like a diet in which you're directed to eat only this or that. You're going to decide—based on what your art map tells you about what you love and need to do—how to craft your hours.

Again, the most important part of this exercise is to build your map around the things that are most meaningful to you, the things that are in your inner circle. Not what's important to me or to your spouse or to your kids or to your boss, but what's important to *you*.

As we noted in the first chapter, life just will not work for us if it's jam-packed with obligations and duties from the outer circle of our map, or with the endless distractions of things that are not meaningful to us at all. We end up becoming angry, agitated, and irritable people with a life like that. And no one is going to make sure we get what we truly need from our inner circle unless we attend to those things ourselves.

We have to show up for our own life. That's the riveting and revealing truth here. No one else will. And, by the way, it's not anyone else's job. It's our job.

I'd like to make that point once again with even more emphasis: No one is going to arrange an art life for us free from duties, distractions, or the daily-ness of life's little details. If we want an art life, then we have to craft it. We have to balance it against work and family and love and all of the annoying and time-killing stuff that needs to get done in a week or a month.

The bottom line is, if we want it, we have to build it.

One of my yoga teachers used to say, "Life doesn't get out of the way so we can get still. We have to learn how to quiet ourselves from the inside out, no matter what is going on around us."

And the same is true for art. Life will not get out of the way for us so that we can create. It will never still or slow down, opening up into endless quiet. We have to *take* the hours we need, craft them, shape them, and get practical about applying ourselves to them. That's the only way our art—and our joy—is ever going to materialize.

"I'm Just Not that Disciplined."

When I talk to artists and would-be artists about creating a time plan, many times the first thing that pops out of their mouths is, "Well, I can't do that. I'm just not that disciplined."

And just like in our financial lives, we artists often cut ourselves off at the knees by saying, "I'm no good with sitting down," or "I started this terrific memoir and I'm just not self-motivated enough to get back to it," or, my personal favorite, "I'm a terrible procrastinator."

And I have news for you: We're *all* terrible procrastinators! We are all paralyzed by fear when we're beginning, and all of us need to learn how to create the structures (i.e., the discipline) to get to the work we really love and to keep returning to it. Each of us has trouble getting started, and trouble continuing, and trouble working steadily through the finish line of a creative piece of work.

That struggle is not particular to you or to any one single artist.

There's a phrase bandied about these days: "Give up your terminal uniqueness." What that means to artists is that we're all human here, and we all face the same kinds of life challenges, in one way or another, to get to our art. So, in order to overcome procrastination and inaction, we have to give up our "specialness" and be willing to take some guidance from others who are already working on their art, who have overcome some of the time obstacles we're dealing with, and then apply some of those same skills to our own life. It means we have to get humble enough to learn how to work regularly; to learn our own form of personal accountability. It means we have to get over ourselves and get down to the thing that's most important: the work.

So, I harken back to the beginning of this book in which we talked about the fact that we were going to have to *learn* the skills of being or becoming a healthy artist. Those skills are not gifted to us. The ability to sit down and really work is absolutely the hardest thing we will ever learn, hands down. That learning curve is not special to you or to me. It's just hard. And we've got to be willing to learn and relearn, finding a way to work, no matter how unprofessional or helpless that makes us feel and no matter how accomplished we think we are or aren't.

We will have to work these skills steadily in slow steps. We need to try out suggestions (from ourselves and from others), and then work on them, let them fail, try something different, fail again, and keep trying until we find something that makes our clock tick. We have to practice the skills of being accountable until something actually kicks the door in and moves us to act. We will not automatically be able to sit down for 10 hours a week and write because we think it's a good idea. In fact, thinking that we "should" will often inhibit us rather than spur us on.

What we're talking about is being willing—willing to try, willing to fail, willing to get up again and then keep getting up again—until we can stand up on our own with strength and balance.

So, give up the nonsense of "I can't be disciplined" and engage in humble exploration. Of course you can learn this. You just need to be shown how.

"No Pessimist Ever Discovered the Secret of the Stars . . ."

Helen Keller once penned a profound thing. She wrote: "No pessimist ever discovered the secret of the stars, or sailed an uncharted land, or opened a new doorway for the human spirit."

What that means to me is, we not only have to give up our specialness, but we also must give up criticism—of ourselves and others—and engage, as best we can, in a daily spirit of discovery.

Pessimism is that nasty drug that we let seep into our veins when we're scared, freaked out, or feeling less-than. We use it as a distancing mechanism—a way to keep the intimacy, vulnerability, and precarious nature of our creativity at arm's length. We particularly use it as a mechanism to promote our own hesitation regarding making time for our art. We criticize ourselves before we even begin, creating a block of "Why try?" that we impose upon ourselves in our panic and fear.

Here's an example of how pessimism works on me. I might

go to an art event, and once inside the door, almost instantly my mind starts spinning out little criticisms of the building, the art, the setup—even the food—just to get a bit of *space* between myself and what other people are creating. The fear is simple: I'm unconsciously measuring myself against other people's work and it's dredging up all kinds of anxiety and angst. And, in the process, I'm dinging my own efforts— particularly related to time—tattling on in my head about how much more I think I should be accomplishing compared to what I'm looking at.

We also use pessimism and criticism to downplay other people's success. In acting circles in Los Angeles in the mid- '90s, there was a certain cache in saying negative things about Meryl Streep's theatrical prowess. "Sure, she's good, but those *accents*! She's so over the top with it!" you'd hear someone say at a party. "I can't stand all of that *expertise*. It's just too much!" someone else might say. And this kind of criticizing won't serve us, either. It's a deflecting tool— trying to hide our envy by denigrating another's work—and it takes us out of our willingness to focus on what we need to do for our own art.

In relation to ourselves, we often use pessimism to trash our early efforts at time management, money clarity, work ethics and motivation—in other words, we speak as if we should already know this stuff, and we ding ourselves for not knowing. And that's not fair. Not to ourselves and not to our artistic impulses. Just listening to what comes out of our mouth about our art and our own self is a huge education. We catch ourselves saying, "I can't," nine times more than we say, "I might be able to." And that's a problem when we're trying to find a way to get to our art.

So, how do we freeze our inner critic and stop the chatter? How can we change the automatic impulse to disparage when we're truly feeling fragile?

I like to think of it this way: The antidote for pessimism, in my opinion, is not optimism. It's not an endless stream of happy thoughts. Life just isn't like that. There are highs and there are lows in life and there's normal human emotion that goes with each. So, the thought that we should always be optimistic is just not workable.

The antidote to pessimism, then, as Helen Keller revealed to us, is *discovery*. It's the willingness to be in the exploration of our creativity, to live in the openness and vulnerability of learning the next thing. Discovery is the bright force that leads our heart out on the open trail of art. It's our own spirit asking us to wake up, to be engaged, and to love the vast, open plain of being called.

It's humbling to discover something. We're learning it as we're finding it. We have to be willing to not know and then be willing to go looking. When we open up to the impulse to discover, it connects us to the living inspiration inside us.

Or, as Jimmy Page so aptly put it in the documentary, *It Might Get Loud*, "The spark had become the flame, and the flame was burning really bright . . ."

So, if that means I have to set aside all of my prejudices

and distancing behaviors just to get myself to let my own spark catch fire and go participate in a songwriting conference, then so be it. If it means I have to *promise myself* that I won't say one negative thing about my art studio, my day job, or how hard it is to submit my new play, then that's what I have to do. If it means I have to catch myself every time I say something negative about my ability to set aside time for my art, or discover what's next, or learn how to manage my money clearly, then I have to gather all my willpower and keep my mouth closed.

When I catch myself making a terrible self-deprecating faux pas, such as, "I should have started when I was 16. Now it's just so arduous," I change tracks as soon as possible and correct myself with something like, "Oops. I take that back. I've got gifts to give *right now* and I can build on them. That's better."

And—surprise, surprise—when I silence my inner critic and make myself willing to learn, I feel more human, more open, and I show up for my art more than when I don't.

Our work building the foundation for our art—getting a day job we can live with, getting money clarity, learning work ethics, mapping an art life and a time plan—builds the bedrock for putting us in touch with our discovery process. And putting our supports into place becomes a discovery in and of itself. Our life will surely change when we employ them; we will get to more of what we love about ourselves, and we will learn great things.

So, get humble, check pessimism at the riverbank, and be

willing to float out into the cool, watery stream of wonder, grace, and discovery by taking your first steps in applying the Time Map we're about to create.

Know Your "Tells."

Before we map our time, we need to talk for a quick moment about distractions.

Distractions, I firmly believe, are blocks we purposely put in the pathway of a creative project because (1) we're afraid what we're about to do won't be "good enough"; (2) we don't know what's coming next creatively or we're terrified nothing inspired will come; or (3) we're resisting the deep, hard work of reworking, rewriting, or reforming our work into something that's professionally ready for the world.

It's a good idea to know, and even list, the things that we will use to distract ourselves from our artwork, particularly when we are about to build an artist's Time Map.

These things are called our "Tells."

In life as well as in art, there are certain *tells*—indicators that we're screwing up, wasting time, or just plain resisting. When I'm in this mode, suddenly the kitchen tile just *has to* get scrubbed, and the bathroom grout is screaming "Clean me now!" Dusting—which I barely ever focus on otherwise—suddenly takes on an urgency not ever known to me at any other time. Straightening the bed, cleaning off nightstands, doing some hand wash—all of this takes on a compelling call to my hands and feet that refuses to let me sit down and write or paint or compose.

These are my own personal tells. When I get obsessed with silly little chores that really don't need doing, it means I'm stalling, dragging my feet, and deep in my own resistance.

Here's my list of time wasters:

- Cleaning (floors, dishes, closets, etc.)
- Scrubbing (tile, bathtub, grout, etc.)
- Rearranging (closet, dishes, shoes, etc.)
- Catch-up phone calls to friends (which I could easily make after working)
- E-mail (a time-sucker like nothing else; can't even open it if I really want to work)
- Facebook, Twitter, Instagram (I have to turn off all devices to overcome these)
- Guitar playing (I can use it as a break between hours of work but not as an excuse to waste time)

And here's the thing all these things have in common, and it's the identifier that these things are my tells: They all require a bit of spin, a torqueing-up of adrenaline, and a (sometimes obsessive) swirling of physical or emotional energy. And my work—writing, painting, or composing—requires just the opposite. It requires stillness. It requires sitting down and getting quiet.

And just because I catch myself in the middle of a tell doesn't mean I can stop the swirling and sit down to work right away. Knowing I'm in resistance helps, but it doesn't necessarily solve it.

Here's what I use to the best of my ability to get myself to stop the spinning and face my creative work. First, I say a little meditation/prayer. I say, out loud, "I'm just the channel for a larger idea. I'm willing to have the power of the idea lead me and use my hands, my heart, my head, and my body in whatever way you—the heart of my idea—ask."

Then I name my favorite great artists, famous and not—out loud—and ask for their help in guiding me. I know that sounds incredibly cosmic and maybe even hokey, but it works for me. It makes me feel I'm standing on the shoulders of other artists who have come before me and who have paved a path that I can walk, too.

Next, I give myself a simple goal—say, a half-hour of work, timed by the timer. I often find that my resistance is bound up in an expectation that everything should happen fast, and that I'm "supposed to" finish gargantuan amounts of work in a blazing timeline. I remind myself that slow, steady steps is the pace at which I'm truly supposed to be moving, and that slow is good. I coach myself down off the wall of resistance by reminding myself that I'm trying to move a glacier here, and I have to chip away at it a pick at a time. In the meantime, I can connect with the beauty of the ice, the solid clink of my hammer against it, and the crisp air around me— my work, step by step and line by line. In other words, when I underexpect, I tend to take the pressure off and it frees me to pay attention, and to really enjoy my work.

When the half-hour is done, I check in with myself. Can I do another half-hour? Am I willing? Then I do another half-hour. I don't do more than an hour on days when I'm truly resistant, because then I won't want to sit down tomorrow. If I feel I need more support, I go for a walking meditation, a half-hour or so in which I think about my piece. Movement dedicated to my art always helps me clarify my work and become more willing.

You'll want to list your own tells, and over time, with the help of the artist's Time Map we're about to make, you'll find your own ways of breaking them. Outing our tells helps us banish the distractions that eat away at our precious art time, and banishing those distractions is how we develop character as artists.

And that, by itself, can change the whole rest of our life.

Allow for Enjoyment.

Many of us find enjoyment in our artwork the minute we're willing to begin it. It feels pleasurable and life-affirming. It's sweet and joyous. It feels real, meaningful, and rich, and we end up proud of our achievements in its world. We might wrestle with our art sometimes, sure; but the wrestling feels worthy—like a good, sweaty workout at the gym.

So, if we truly do love our artwork, why does it seem to take an act of God for us to get back to our workbench and work on it?

Here's why. We are not skilled in enjoyment in our life. We are skilled in fielding immediate needs, addressing weighty responsibilities, and attending to pressing duties. We feel guilty about giving ourselves art time. And as psychologically simplistic as that sounds, most of us have at least a bucketful or more of this guilt rambling around in our head and heart. We're afraid that if we give ourselves over to our art, we'll somehow become irresponsible and let the rest of our life fall apart.

And we have to just give that up—before we begin crafting the art map of our week's timeline. Otherwise we will not offer ourselves the hours we truly need. We'll shortchange ourselves if we work from guilt, and we'll create more frustration in our life instead of less.

If we pray or meditate, we can ask to have this guilt lifted. If we believe in the power of growth or love at all, we can humble ourselves before that growth and ask of ourselves to have anything that does not serve our life removed. We can ask our own heart to be stronger, to be braver, and to open up to better and happier emotions.

What we are practicing by using the tools in this book is *balance*. We're not advocating a throw-over-all-your-responsibilities-to-get-to-your-art experience. We are not promoting an all-or-nothing approach. So, we can stop thinking that our art will make us irresponsible, negligent, or rash. That's what this whole book is about: being a responsible, balanced, attentive person who makes art. Art does not rank 5th or 10th or 20th on our list of priorities. It is not hidden on the back shelf of our closet. But it also doesn't engulf or blot out our responsibilities. In our approach, it is established in balance.

Knowing that we're setting up a well-balanced life, we can give up guilt forever. We can banish it. It has no place in our life, and we have no need for it anymore. We are showing up for *all* of it—a whole and full life. We are attending to everything we need to attend to: our God-given talent, our unreplicated gifts, our loving relationships, our family life, our day job, our money, and our time.

And there's nothing more powerful than that kind of conscious action. And we get to own that. We are creating a conscious life.

This foundation in balance gives us every right to our own enjoyment, every right to our art. So, please take this to heart as we begin to craft our artist's Time Map. You're doing the work, so you deserve the joy.

Get Time Clarity with an "Overall."

So, let's get down to it. Let's get ourselves an example of an artist's Time Map.

First and foremost, as has been said before, your Time Map will be your own, with input from only you. No one is going to tell you what you're supposed to do. You're going to craft this, and you're in charge.

What we're looking for here is—just like with our

money—personal clarity with our time. Where can we carve out hours for art? Where can we still and quiet the stuff that doesn't matter and put art in its place? How can we create an art schedule that's balanced with all of the other things we have to do in a week or a month?

Be brutally honest with yourself as you begin. Don't plot a plan that looks amazing but is unworkable for your life. Don't make a pie-in-the-sky schedule that slams you to the mat in the first week of using it, which then makes you give up before you even get going.

Think: balance. Think: slow, steady steps.

A good rule of thumb is *underwhelm yourself.* Especially at the beginning. What we're after is the sensation of getting up on our first wobbly waterski, and then the next one, just getting the feel of the bank of water pressing against our legs. We want to start developing the muscles to stand up strongly atop the waves of our time pressures.

The first thing we're going to do is map the "Overall" of our week. Take out a good-size sheet of paper. (I like to do this on paper, so I can scribble notes, versus do it on a screen, but do what works for you.) Then, divide your week into "fixed hours"—hours that are scheduled for you already, such as day job-hours—and "flex hours," which are not prescheduled. You'll absolutely forget some things that take up time the first time around, but don't get upset. Just adjust as things come up.

Here is an example of an "Overall" for an artist who I worked with who has a job, a husband, and two kids to raise:

SUZETTE'S "OVERALL"

FIXED HOURS

Morning school routine	6:30 a.m.–8:00 a.m.
Take kids to school	8:00 a.m.–8:30 a.m.
Commute	8:30 a.m.–9:00 a.m.
Day job	9:00 a.m.–5:00 p.m.
Commute	5:00 p.m.–5:45 p.m.
Dinner/kids' homework	6:00 p.m.–7:30 p.m.

FLEX HOURS

Lunch hour	12:30 p.m.–1:00 p.m.
Weeknights	7:30 p.m.–11:00 p.m.
Friday eves	7:30 p.m.–12:00 a.m.
Saturday	8:00 a.m.–11:00 p.m.
Sunday	8:00 a.m.–10:00 p.m.

We can see from this quick "Overall" approach just where Suzette's hours are blocked out with responsibilities and just how much time her day job takes each week. Suzette is a visual artist, crafting exquisite glass art on large wooden canvas surfaces, and, lucky for her, her day job as a curriculum coordinator at a local middle school is steady but not high pressure. She likes her job, so she doesn't need to spend the time to change it to something easier on the soul. But because she has two kids, a marriage to nurture, and a house to help maintain, she has a lot on her plate.

By looking at her "Overall," we can see where her flexible hours are. Certainly, we understand that there are many more duties that have to be covered by Suzette's flex hours than just her art—particularly since she is a parent and a partner in a relationship. And our goal is to address all of them. To balance each need with her call to make art.

Remember, in our money plan, we divided our spending into a Bills and a Daily Needs section, both of which we could adjust or downsize depending on the cuts we were willing to make. The same is true with our time. We each will have fixed hours and flex hours. Although it's harder to adjust our fixed hours, it's still very possible with some dedicated effort.

But our immediate goal is to massage the obvious flex hours we have to serve us artistically. We are looking to craft a Time Map that works for us for *exactly how things are now*. Should we choose to make bigger changes in our fixed hours—for instance, by changing jobs so we can work less, downsizing our day-job hours and our monthly spending to live on less—we can do that later. Right now, we're working on the skill of getting to our artwork in whatever ways we can, and as immediately as possible.

So, don't wait until you have the perfect day job or your life "calms down" after the kids' soccer season is over. Just begin now with what you have.

That's our objective. We're going to start now and begin practicing the skills of working our art on a regular basis.

The Nuts and Bolts of Your Artist's "Time Map."

So, let's take look at what Suzette did to build regular art hours into her schedule by using the tool of the artist's Time Map.

There are a few principles she needed to employ here, based on the nature of her artwork. Since Suzette works in a large format, and constructs with cut glass, she needed more than half-hour art sessions to make her art time meaningful and accomplishment-oriented, and still clean up and leave her work area safe.

As we worked together, I noticed that she had half-hour lunch breaks, but she tended to work right through them, never leaving her desk. I asked her to change that, and to use that time to get out of the office to sketch for 10 to 15 minutes or read something related to her art while she's eating. That meant she had to pack her lunch—no running out to grab something at the burrito spot. Changing her lunchtime routine also saved her quite a bit of money each month—cash she could put toward art supplies without changing anything else in her family's spending plan.

Next, she needed to address a time issue setting up her art space. In the past, she would take over one corner of the family room to work, and since it took so much time to set up and break down her supplies and art tools, she ended up not working, leaving her stuff packed up in the garage. Her space issues were a deterrent to getting to her art, and since she couldn't afford a studio, she felt boxed in.

With a little negotiation with her family, she agreed to set up her art "studio" in the garage. That meant she and her husband had to park their cars in the driveway so she could work—a small price to pay for her happiness, she realized. Suzette took one Saturday afternoon and moved all of the family's sporting gear to one corner of the garage, then set up her workspace. Her objective was to be able to leave her work out—to not have to pack it up after she was through with an art session—so she could get back to it more quickly. Since she works with glass and has kids, she got a locksmith to install a new lock on the door, and only she and her husband have access to the keys.

Next, she wanted to find a few hours a week for courting professionalism in her work. The most direct way to do that was to take class at the local community college or the art conservatory and get some critical input and instruction. She and her husband agreed that they would each take one night a week for a project or cause they were passionate about, and on the alternate evening, each would take on kids, dinner, homework, and baths solo. This freed Suzette up to take a conservatory class one evening a week, and ended up doing much more than that: It gave her a much-needed break from family duties and being a mom. She came back to her family after class with her energy fully spent, surely, but feeling excited and nurtured as well.

So, let's go over the Time Map she created. Again, I like to do mine on a big sheet of paper with pencil, so I can erase and draw on it, but do what is best for you. Here we've used a table created in Microsoft Word, divided in two: one for weekdays, and one for weekends.

WEEKDAYS

	MONDAY	TUESDAY	WEDNESDAY	THURSDAY	FRIDAY
6:30–8:00	Morning routine	Morning routine	Morning routine	Morning routine	Morning routine
8:00–8:30	Kids to school	Kids to school	Kids to school	Kids to school	Kids to school
8:30–9:00	Commute	Commute	Commute	Commute	Commute
9:00–12:30	Job	Job	Job	Job	Job
12:30–1:00	Eat/sketch Get out of office	Eat/sketch Get out of office	Eat/sketch Get out of office	Eat/sketch Get out of office	Eat/sketch Get out of office
1:00–5:00	Job	Job	Job	Job	Job
5:00–6:00	Commute	Commute	Commute	Commute	Commute
6:00–7:30	Dinner Kids' homework	ART CLASS	Dinner Kids' homework	Dinner Kids' homework	Dinner Kids' homework
7:30–8:00	Exercise walk w/ family	ART CLASS	Exercise walk w/ family	Rick's night out	Date night with Rick
8:00–9:00	TV/relax	ART CLASS	TV/relax	TV/relax	
10:00	Bedtime Read/ journal	Drive home from art class	Bedtime Read/ journal	Bedtime Read/ journal	Bedtime Read/ journal
10:30		Home from class/ bed			

Since Suzette's weekdays are already very packed with family and job responsibilities, her goal was to add art anyplace she could. Note that by working her Time Map, she was able to add 15 minutes of sketching a day, Monday through Friday, and added an art class which gave her adult time to work on art in the company of other artists. She was able to add 4 hours and 15 minutes of art to her busy week, just by reprioritizing and making some simple shifts. She could also write for a few minutes at bedtime about her art and sketch little ideas in her journal. And, because she made the hugely helpful decision to turn her garage into her studio, she opened up the opportunity for productive weekend art hours that she could plan for or add depending on her family's schedule.

Her plan also helped her set aside some dedicated time to be with her husband, coordinating an every Friday night "date." Their dates might be as simple as a drink at the local trattoria around the corner, but it worked to help them get some romantic reconnection after the week.

Note that since she had agreed with herself to sketch 15 minutes a day, if she misses it one day for some reason, she owes herself that 15 minutes some other time in the week—meaning she might have to get up a half-hour early one morning and put in her time. If she skips her three weekend hours on Saturday—which we're about to discuss—she's got to get up especially early the next day and put in those hours.

That's the work ethic that we're trying to employ, so we always feel good about showing up for our art.

Now let's take a look at her weekends:

WEEKENDS

	SATURDAY		SUNDAY
6:30–8:00	Sleep in	6:30–8:00	Sleep in
8:00–12:00	Kids' Sports events	8:00–10:00	ARTWORK
1:00–1:30	Drive home from events	10:00–4:30	Family time
1:30–4:30	ARTWORK	4:30–5:30	ARTWORK–FLEX
6:00–9:00	Dinner with family or events, socializing, invitations, extended family, etc.	6:00 – 9:00	Dinner with family
9:00–11:00	TV/relax	9:00–10:00	TV/relax/read

Note that, in Suzette's weekend Time Map, she purposely made no commitments or plans for Saturday evenings. Since Friday evenings were set aside for her husband, she needed a flexible night to attend or plan family events, parties, holidays, events, and accept invitations. A free Saturday night worked to attend to those other obligations.

With her husband, Rick's agreement, she went into her studio every Saturday *for three solid hours*, morning or afternoon, depending on her kids' sports schedule. If her kids had an event in the morning, she worked in the afternoon. If they had a game in the afternoon, she worked in the morning. She and Rick agreed that if the kids' sporting events happened on both weekend days, she would only attend one day, putting in her art hours on the other.

She calendared her hours by Wednesday of each week,

and posted them on the fridge, so everyone would know when she'd be committed. When she was working on her canvasses, no one in the family was allowed to interrupt her. No knocking on the door, no "Where's my football jersey?" no phone calls or questions—just radio silence for three solid hours. That also meant that as the family was getting used to this arrangement, Suzette had to set clear parameters and not give in to interruptions. If a knock on the door came, she didn't answer it, at all, period. No yelling back—just no response. It was a gentle but firm way of letting everyone know that she meant business. She had a lock on the door and used it. After a few tries, the kids got the message and went and asked their dad for help. And she had to train her husband, too. Putting her headset in her ears and turning up some music helped her not hear anything but her own thoughts so she could get to her work.

Once her family figured out that she was happier and more relaxed when she did her creative work, their support came without resistance. In fact, when she was crabby from time to time, her oldest son would say to her, "Mom, you need to go work on your art."

Beyond her solid three-hour Saturday commitment, she added two hours on Sunday morning, a time when the kids and her husband were usually watching sports or movies. It was dead time for her, and she realized she could use it to work. From 8:00 to 10:00 a.m. every Sunday, she went into the garage, locked the door, and crafted her art. If there was nothing much going on in the family's day, she could also slip back into her art space before dinner and work for another hour. The flex times also gave her an opportunity to make up some hours in those weeks where everything went to hell, and her planned schedule got dinged.

By mapping her art hours, she was able to give herself five to six hours of art every weekend, plus just over four hours during the week, as well as some artistic journaling time on weekday nights. These were real chunks of time that were incredibly meaningful to her and her art. After just two months, she had completed two medium-size canvasses and had made some real progress on her huge one. She felt better about herself, more inspired about her life, and grateful and happy in her family.

That's what we're after: satisfaction, in the most expansive sense of the word. And our artist's Time Map helps us get there.

Working Your Map in the Real World.

You may think by reading the previous section that Suzette wrote out her Time Map and then—*ba-boom!*—she was instantly willing to sit down and do her artwork in her allotted hours.

And that's not the way it works. It didn't work that way for her, or for me, or for anyone else I know who has used this method.

When we're beginning and we're still swirling inside with

our "I'm not good enough," "I'm not disciplined enough," or "I'll never get over my procrastination" thoughts, we're not usually going to be able to implement our Time Map right out of the gate, or just because we wrote it down. We're going to have to fail at using our map at least a few times—and maybe even a dozen times—before we find out what works for us. Yes, it's incredibly useful to see where we *can* map some hours for art, but that doesn't mean we *will* use them for art. So, don't think that because you crafted a time plan and you know it's a good idea, you'll instantaneously know how to work with it.

Just like the spending plan, it's takes about three months to get the gist of using the thing. And we want to give ourselves a break as we figure it out and work the map, and not throw the baby out with the bathwater. Meaning, just because it doesn't work the first or second time, doesn't mean it won't work for you eventually.

The artist's Time Map is a *guide*, plain and simple. That's why we work into it flex times, buffer zones with no scheduled activities, and open-ended areas, so that we can recover hours for art when our resistance has gotten the best of us. It's going to happen. We will find ourselves roaming the aisles of our local home goods store rather than doing our art. We are going to catch ourselves surfing the net for new boots instead of working. We'll vacuum, scrub, clean out, or reorganize something—anything—instead of sitting down to create.

And, it's also absolutely certain that something will come up to distract or destroy our art hours beyond our own resistance. The outside world is like that: It tends to dump stuff on our heads that clamors for our instant attention. No big deal. It happens to all of us. So, just accept it and know that overcoming all of that is part of the learning curve. Failing is part of the nature of acquiring new skills and employing something new. Don't take it personally. Just get back up and try again.

When you're just learning how to work the Time Map, my best advice is to use a timer. Don't schedule any more than three hours of art at a time at the beginning, and less is better. We're not after one long day of art and then no art for days on end. We're after regularity with our art practice.

What I like to do is set the timer for an hour, and click it off and reset it for every hour that I complete. If my goal is two hours of writing, I set the timer, click it off for each hour, and give myself the dignity of knowing I'm completing my work as I go. (One note about timers: Don't use your phone timer if you have a tendency to pick up phone calls, texts, or e-mails when you're supposed to be working. Turn the thing OFF. The world will not disintegrate and your family will not fall apart if you can't be reached for two hours.)

It can also be helpful to print out your Time Map so you can make notes in the margins about what worked and what didn't. I got myself a gold marking pen, and for the first few months when I did my hours, I put a simple star on my artist Time Map. Then, at the end of a couple of weeks, I'd check to see what needed tweaking.

So, be flexible with your Time Map. Adjust. Try again and adjust again. Don't hold your heart to the fire with a lot of self-flagellation if you didn't get to the hours you mapped out. Just keep tweaking until you find a schedule that starts to work.

Just like getting a day job you can live with, this effort deserves some of your sweat and blood. It's the foundation upon which you will build the whole of your art life, for the rest of your life. So, take some time with it over the course of a few months, and keep experimenting.

If you can't get started the first week, try again the second week. If you stare at your writing notebook and barely write a few lines of poetry in your allotted time, but you've shown up and clicked off your hours, then give yourself credit. Our goal is to keep trying and keep working until we've built some real and formidable artistic strength. We're looking for bedrock here—something solid to stand upon, not just for today, but for a lifetime.

Over time, we will intuitively know when to show up for our art the way we know when to show up for our day job. We won't even have to look at our Time Map.

Remember, though, for most of us, we're just at the beginning of learning these skills. We are building our art muscles, day in and day out, until we've got some seriously strong artistic biceps to push ourselves up with.

What to Do if You Have a Crazy Schedule.

So, let's say you're willing to craft a Time Map but your schedule changes from week to week. Or you've got a day job that requires you to work wacky hours—early mornings and late nights at random intervals. What then?

Here's what to do. If you get a new schedule from your employer every week (as restaurant workers do), then as soon as you get it, sit right down and map out a quick Time Map for the week. Knowing your time goals cold helps with this a lot. For instance, if you know you want to put in four hours a week on your giant quilted canvas, you'll take a look at your new weekly schedule, and map out when you can put in those four hours. You can write your schedule on a napkin if you have to and keep it in your wallet, put it in your Notes app on your phone, or use the same notebook you're using for your money: It doesn't matter. The object is to map your art time the minute you get your schedule for the week. Don't wait or you won't do your art. Write it up the moment you know which hours you have free.

What if you have wildly different hours and it affects your ability to work well? I have this challenge. Some days I'm up at 5:45 a.m. to teach yoga, and other days I have evening classes that put me home close to 10 at night. And though my schedule is fairly stable from week to week, I have a very physical job and it affects my ability to work clearheadedly on my art.

So, here's what we do in that situation. We note the hours that are most productive and schedule our art hours in those blocks of time. Again, we may be working with two-hour blocks—which is truly time enough for some serious accomplishment—and we schedule our work on those days and times when we work best.

And note that when you work best may change. I always *think* I should be writing in the morning, but often *do* write in the afternoon—particularly after I have exercised in some way. In the end, it doesn't really matter what I think works best. It matters what actually *does* work best. So, I have to observe, note, and be willing to try things out. That's what the Time Map helps me to do.

The point is to not let a changing or variable schedule stop us from working a Time Map and getting to our art.

Learn What Works for You.

My husband offers this advice to his creative writing students: "If it's possible for you to do your creative work first thing in the morning, then do it. Then, no matter what happens in the hours that follow, you own the day. You know that if the winds blow and the skies rumble, you were building the pyramids just this morning—and no one can take that away from you."

Maybe dragging yourself out of bed at 5:30 a.m. will be harder than hell to begin with, but then once you're up, you notice that you get terrific work done in the quiet of the morning and end up feeling great about yourself. That's the approach of doing your artwork first. It's the "pay yourself first" idea, and it's a very solid way to work your artistic Time Map.

But getting up extra early to compose or sculpt or write for an hour won't work for everyone. So, you've got to adjust your timeline to your own life and its cycles. As Anne Lamott advises, "Give up the ten o'clock news . . . [it's only going] to tell you about fires in areas you never go to." Do your art instead. Take an hour, in reasonably regular increments, and get your hands in your work.

Remember that we don't get up one day and—*ta-dah!*—decide to run a marathon. We train for it. We go out on the road over and over, day after day—through rain and heat and humidity—and keep trekking along. That's why the mapping idea is so powerful. It makes us take a look at where we could be making art. It lets us in on the fact that we can make a simple shift here or there and apply ourselves, in small steps, to our passions.

We also have to give up thinking that we're not professional or "real" artists if we only sit down for half an hour a day. As I mentioned before, I have a dear friend who writes children's books and keeps a day job at a Trader Joe's market. He gets two 15-minute breaks a day, and uses each to go outside, sit on a bench, and write. That's a half-hour of writing every day. And over the course of a month or two, he gets a significant amount of story down on the page.

So, if all you can do is sketch for 15 minutes on weekdays and set aside two hours for your art on the weekend, by the end of a single year, you'll end up with quite a body of work to share. As I said before, I wrote my entire first book by writing one hour a day, four days a week, and completed it in just over a year and a half.

Our object is to set small time goals and get ourselves

inside our art regularly—and then cheer for ourselves and reward ourselves with the pride that we deserve for our accomplishments.

Set Boundaries.

One of things I notice when working with artists who say they can't find time for their artwork is they often have not learned how to set boundaries in their day-job life. And though the phrase *set boundaries* has been terribly overused, it fits well here, and it's an important part of being able to work our Time Map and get to our art.

Certainly we could have talked about this issue in the day job chapter, but we're talking about it here because we need to address the things that prevent us from working our Time Map—and a boundaryless work environment is the prime culprit.

Many, many American employers have gotten into the nasty habit of expecting their employees to *not* take lunch breaks, *not* take vacation time due them, and to stay late and arrive early for no particular reason other than the fact that they've set up a workaholic work environment. This will not work in an artist's life.

Most of us have worked for such bosses: people who have no home life and no particular social life, or who hang out in front of their computer screens for hours on end and then expect those who work under them to do the same.

Second, there are those of us who work at jobs that we once thought would be good for our art—part-time, home-based work, for instance—who end up doing twice the work for half the pay, and are not able to extricate ourselves from the constant phone calls and extra labor. Fundraising and event-planning gigs for low-paying nonprofits are a prime example of this kind of thing. We get into a "need-to-be-needed" cycle, and in the end, we have no particular hours. We're just at the beck and call of our employer. This will not work, either.

So, how do we negotiate the land of employers who are not healthy and not balanced regarding their work life and their impact on ours? How do we institute what we need for a balanced art life?

First, we have to speak up. We have to understand that *we teach people how to treat us*. If we've done a poor job of that so far, we can learn the skills to draw stronger lines in the sand about what we will and won't do. Know this: We are obliged to put in a good day's work. We are not obliged to be run ragged by our employer so that the rest of our life is blotted out.

When interviewing or setting boundaries with an employer, you can use these words: "I'd like you to know that I take my lunch hours, I take my vacations, and I expect to accomplish my work in an eight-hour day and then go home. I believe that a balanced life creates a more productive worker."

As my dad used to say, "If you can't get your work done in an eight-hour day, you're doing something wrong."

Several years ago I had a day job that I needed desperately—
it was just after I had fallen on my face with debt and had lost
my entire income source, and I was starting all over—and
still, even when I was desperate, I set those boundaries. I did
it nicely, but I did it.

On the first day of my employment, I brought my lunch,
closed my office door, and put up a Post-it that said, "Lunch
1:00–2:00 p.m." I ate, read my book, and then went out walking for a half-hour. In the next week or two, our administrative assistant popped her head in about five different times to
tell me I had a call during my break, and I very nicely told her
I'd get back to the caller after my lunch hour. After that she
stopped coming in and sent the calls to voice mail. I'm certain
that everyone thought I was a little nuts.

But here's what happened. The culture in our office was
that everyone ate lunch at their desk and kept working. After
about two months, I noticed other people closing their door
and leaving "At lunch" Post-it notes on them, too. And the
sky did not fall. Everyone respected the lunch notes, and
we each very gracefully claimed the rest time due us. It was
an amazing example of how a simple nonverbal boundary
changed an entire work environment.

Beyond breaks, there are those employers who thrive
on adrenaline—they have a never-ending series of
"emergencies"—many of which occur at 4:45 p.m., and some
due to their own poor planning, for which you "must" stay
late. In these instances, the best advice I can offer is that you
must throw an elbow at least once. Meaning, you'll have to

get up the strength to assess the need, and if it's truly not life-threatening to the company, tell your boss you'll be in at 9:00 the next morning, you'll be able to address the issue then, and go home. Leave. Don't discuss it and don't hang around to field objections. Just go.

I once had a grant-writing client who called me at all hours of the day and expected me to pick up the phone. Most often, the two directors just wanted to gripe, or chat, or swirl themselves into a lather over their money panic, and after about three months, I noticed I was spending hours talking them both down off the wall. Since they were on the East Coast and I was on the West Coast, they'd call at 9:00 a.m. their time—6:00 a.m. for me—and expect me to jump out of bed, run in to my office, and take the call. Worse than that, I had mountains of writing to do for them, and they were taking up hours of my part-time commitment *kvetching*.

What I finally did was tell the director I'd be available one hour a day for calls related to grants, from 1:00 to 2:00 p.m. Eastern, and I'd field whatever else they needed by e-mail and respond the next day. I explained to her that I wasn't getting enough dedicated writing time—which was my job—and very nicely set a boundary. They stopped calling except during the hours set and stopped complaining as much. If they happened to get adrenalized about some issue or another, calling me in an off-hour, their call went straight to voice mail. Most important, I stopped codependently trying to field their angst, by not picking up the phone except during my allotted communication hours.

All of this speaks to the quality of your day job. Sometimes you can work with your day-job employer by setting your own boundaries and by teaching people how to treat you. Know that it will take everyone in your environment at least a few weeks to get used to your new limits, but they will adjust. When you set them with kindness and firmness your work environment will most often shift and improve.

But if it doesn't, then it's time to go back to the drawing board and find a day job you can live with. Complaining and complaining about a day job that's sucking up your time only creates suffering, and as we said before, suffering will not work in the life of an artist.

If you're the one who's cycling on adrenaline, overworking a day job during your supposed-to-be-for-art hours, then get help. Truly, go to an artist's support group, or a free 12-step group, such as Debtor's Anonymous (which addresses the issue of "time-debting"), or get a counselor, coach, or friend to help you.

Our time is precious as artists, and learning to set boundaries is the only thing that will help us claim it, own it, and begin to use it well.

Get Support.

For some reason—and maybe it's because, for a lot of us, our artistic expression requires working solo—we forget to compare notes with other artists. We forget to ask those who are more practiced than we are how they got into the habit of working regularly on their art.

And we miss a wealth of support by not reaching out.

A lot of artists enjoy talking about their process. Some don't, obviously, but we can usually find someone in our immediate realm who we can reach out to and ask how they approach their work. We're particularly looking for someone who may be a bit farther down the road than we are with using time well and honoring his or her art hours.

Reaching out to another artist can be incredibly uplifting. First, we realize that we're not the only ones who have trod this road, and by reaching out, we notice that we're not alone on our path. And that's a great thing all by itself.

So, let's say we've found someone to reach out to. What are we after?

Think of it like doing an informational interview. If you were writing a short article on an artist's work ethics, what would be helpful to ask? You may want to know how this person got started, how they come back to artwork after being away from it for a while, how they motivate themselves. You may ask what's difficult and what's gotten easier with practice. You may want to know what they've done to recover after a loved project didn't lift off the ground; how they found confidence again to begin a new project. You may want to know how they map their time specifically, and how they've overcome distractions.

I find it most useful to compare notes with other artists who have day jobs, so that the sharing is realistically aligned with my own life. I'm not looking to reach out to some hugely successful celebrity: That will get me nowhere. I want to talk to working artists who have the same challenges that I do, who may offer me something real that I can implement in my own daily life.

I once wrote a page-long (and probably overly sincere) letter to a successful writer who had written a small volume on artistic motivation, asking him how he balanced his life with his art and how I could balance mine. I was vulnerable and let him know that I was struggling, and that I needed help figuring this out for myself. After several weeks, he did respond, but he blew my question off in a single sentence, saying he could not help. He was right. He didn't help. It was not useful, and, in fact, it hurt a bit. That's not what we're after when we go looking for support. We need to be reasonably sure when we reach out that the person we're reaching toward will take our need for answers seriously and will care enough about us to respond kindly.

I have also learned the hard way to stay away from conversations with other artists who are trying to impress me or need to prove themselves in some public or I'm-more-successful-than-you-are, showy way. And there's a lot of insecurity out there in the world of artists, so we have to learn to steer our ship away from those people as quickly as humanly possible.

What we're after is sincere sharing with someone whom we're fairly sure will respond generously, vulnerably, and humbly. We want someone who knows what we know: That it's about the work, not the hype. We're looking for any honest connection we can make with another artist who gets where we are, what we're up against, and can offer some real-world encouragement and inspiration.

So, reach out and talk to other artists. We need all the tools we can get our hands on to work with our Time Map and build our work ethics. When we're willing to stand on the shoulders of those who have gone before us and receive some honest help, our artist's path gets less lonely and so much easier to walk.

A Last Look at Time Guidelines.

Last but not least, we are going to review what we talked about in the "Master Your Time" chapter on how to stay *in* while we're working. I call it my "Unsurpassed Time Guidance List," a simple list of things to help keep us on track once we've set aside our time and sit down to do our work.

First, our objective is to set aside a reasonable chunk of time and calendar it. That's what the "Overall" and the artist's Time Map will help us do.

Second, in order to really work on our art, we have to banish distractions during our allotted time. That means we can't make *any* other plans when we schedule our art hours. We don't answer the phone and we turn all nearby phones *off* at least 10 minutes before we're scheduled to begin. We don't text, we don't open e-mail, and we don't open the computer at all for any other use than for art (for instance, if we write or compose music on our computers). We turn off *all* alarms and noise notifications on all devices. This sets the stage for uninterrupted exploration, for the quiet that's necessary to listen to our own ideas.

Next, we don't engage in little errands, household cleanup, or little fixes—that is, we don't do "this one little thing" when it's our art time. Instead, we sit down.

When we think of what we want to accomplish in a particular hour, session, week, or month, we underwhelm ourselves. We assess what we think we can get done in the chunk of time we have and then cut it by two-thirds. Why? Because almost all things take three times longer than we estimate. So, we save ourselves grief by giving ourselves more time to create instead of less.

What we're after is breathing room—time to explore. We remember that the creative act is unlike anything else we do. It requires nonlinear, uninterrupted open space in our head and heart. So, we give ourselves the dignity of taking slow, steady steps. We don't rush. We try our best not to push harder or work longer under the belief that this will make us succeed faster. We work on our art at a normal, human pace and live our life in the meantime.

We practice trust. Meaning, we build our confidence by working our art Time Map, knowing that there will be more time later on: tomorrow, the next day, next week, and next month. Crazy pressure will not feed our inspiration and willingness; room to create will.

We remember always that slow, regular work hours get

much more accomplished than big bursts. For example, a half-hour a day of artwork, five days a week, produces a significant amount of output over a six-month period.

When we work at a normal pace we give ourselves the dignity of a *life* while we're creating. We rid ourselves of outcome expectations. We practice detachment. We learn to work for the joy of having our hands in our art. What we're after is a work ethic that gets us into the delight of our artistry over and over again, no matter what the outcome of a particular piece.

We give ourselves credit for every hour we put in. If it's a gold star on our Time Map that's going to make us feel like a champ, then we buy ourselves a box of stick-on gold stars and paste them on for every hour we work. If it's leaving a text on our best friend's phone that reads, "Did my three hours," then we do it. Whatever it takes to give ourselves the appreciation we deserve for honoring our work ethic and putting in our hours is what we give ourselves.

We work our art muscles until they are so strong that we do our art no matter what else is going on. We return to it again and again, like a friend we're dying to visit with, or a lover we're longing to get alone in the bedroom.

Lastly, we remember that as an artist we walk in praise of beauty—the beauty of being in touch with our own inspiration, willingness, and creative bravery, and the exquisiteness of bringing our gifts out into the world.

I found this quote in a liturgical prayer book that sums it up perfectly: "We pray to break the bonds that keep us from the world of beauty . . . We pray that we may walk in a garden of purpose, in touch with the power of the world."

That is what we get when we show up for our art. And all of that beauty will move mountains in our mind, our heart, our body, and our life.

7:

MOTIVATE YOURSELF

When You Can't Stuff It Anymore....

Most of the time the reason we won't be able to stuff our art anymore won't be because we're bursting with readiness and confidence—it will be because we *have to* do it or we'll mess up our lives, our health, or our well-being.

The most world-rocking thing we need to learn about our artistry is that pushing it away will not lead to happiness.

Avoiding the hard climb up the mountain by filling our days with piles of meaningless minutia that we don't care about just won't do it. Continuing to toil in the land of business while ignoring the press of our creativity will not solve it. Diverting ourselves with the importance of family life, volunteer work, or any other cause, and not setting aside time for our art, will not—no matter how much we hype ourselves with the "importance" of those things—work.

In fact, without our art, our life will tend to tank in the opposite direction, toward restlessness, agitation, nonspecific anxiety, and—let's just say it—bitchiness.

When we don't do our art, we're pissed for no discernible reason. We spout a rolling commentary on what's wrong with the world, on what's not working globally and personally, and we become an epicenter of dissatisfaction. We're like decomposing compost inside: We keep putting scraps in the bin and expecting it to smell sweet.

And—as Steven Pressfield wrote in his terrific book *The War of Art*—we then start to develop *symptoms*.

I can tell every time I'm in the company of an artist who has not begun her work or has not found the discipline to continue something he started. There's an agitated, ground-level anger or dissatisfaction emanating from the person—a palpable unhappiness seeping out, as if discontent had become stuck to the skin. There'll be menial little health problems. There'll be low-level relationship angst and regrets about the past. There'll be out-of-whack frustration over stupid stuff, depression, and malaise when there's nothing really wrong.

But here's the good news: When we hit that pissy-angry, vaguely depressive point, we can train ourselves to use it as a touchstone, a beacon for knowing the truth about where we are with our art. We are at the end of our rope with our procrastinating, and the only thing that's going to fix it is to use the tools we're talking about in this book to *sit down and do what we need to do.*

Cultivate a Good Attitude.

I used to have a goofy acting coach who, before every audition reading or monologue, made the entire class chant,

"*What* are we? *What* are we? We're happy to be here; easy to work with!"

And that should be the spirit that we take into our exploration of how best to motivate ourselves in our work. It's a happy discovery—a discovery we're glad to be a part of and glad to be in the middle of.

We're not looking to be the kind of artists who lead with what's wrong, who grumble about how hard it is to be creative, or who always have some negative thing to carp about. That's not going to get us anywhere. Sure, we're going to have bad days—everyone does—and we're gentle with ourselves when we have them. But we're not looking to *lead* with what's worst about our artist's life.

We're looking to cultivate a good attitude.

So, what's a "good attitude" and how do we get one?

First off, we watch what's coming out of our mouth to friends and acquaintances. We don't wallow in self-pity. We don't start conversations with what's most arduous. We don't piss and moan about other peoples' successes, or about the global lack of supports for artists or the hellish uphill battles we have to walk just to eke out a little creativity. We give up *griping*.

Next, we find joy in the simple things. A good day's work. A completed project. A feeling of accomplishment that we're working on the things that we say are truly important to us. A sensation of being more connected in our relationships because we're not dissatisfied with our own selves. We build on the knowledge that when we're 90, we won't look back with bitter regret and say, "Why didn't I have the courage to try to do my art?"

We are offering our hearts to something that's meaningful and we hold that as valuable and speak about it like it is. We *claim* the good of being an artist for ourselves.

In other words, we cultivate the exact attitude of "Happy to be here, easy to work with!" A good attitude makes us feel better and makes us easier to be around, which is worth the effort all by itself.

Think Like an Inventor.

Inventions—which is what we're working with as artists—don't usually pop into the material world fully formed. They have to be thought out, tinkered with, built, manipulated, reworked, and dreamed over—time and time again—in each progressive stage along the way. They need room to breathe and grow and find things in themselves through us. Meaning, we are only the channel through which creativity speaks. *So, we have to motivate ourselves to show up long enough to be spoken through.*

As ethereal as that sounds, every creative person, scientist, author, or inventor I've known or have read about talks about the process of setting aside time, then "getting out of the way" and obeying the creative call. That's the payoff of putting time aside for our art: Our own inner guidance finds us and speaks to us.

In the day to day, though, inventing feels a lot less simple than just "obeying the call" and listening for our inspirational voices. It's almost never a woke-up-inspired-and-wrote-it-down-in-one-full-piece experience.

So, we have to give up thinking of creativity as magic dust—as fully formed art that springs forth completely birthed, grown up, and polished. What we do instead is begin to take pleasure in the discovery. We can learn to think like the great sculptors who saw the shape of the to-be-carved form in the rock, and then, like they did, patiently chisel away at the stone, one pick stroke at a time. We can learn to think like the scientists who have given up the concept of matter and who play with the nature of light waves, not knowing what they may discover. This is what it means to *invent*. We give up the myth of instantaneous knowing and work anyway, unravelling, uncovering, and unveiling, moving back and forth between the form and the formless, living inside the incredible grace of our inventing power.

We take to heart what Thomas S. Kuhn said in his powerful book *The Structure of Scientific Revolution*: That is, it takes numerous blunders before we work through our old ways of seeing and create a new paradigm.

We work with the beautiful sentiment that the American poet Charlie Smith shared in his poem "Indistinguishable from the Darkness"—that is, "The way out is through." And we keep working, even when we can't yet see where we are going.

In other words, our motivation needs to come from the knowledge that are absolute inventors. Be it in color, structure, shape, texture, word, image, sound, or lyric, we are inventing and creating a new form, a new vision, and new delights for the soul. And we must hold ourselves in that light, patiently willing to let our visions unfold.

Do Your Art Because It's Worth Doing.

The worthiness of my artistic efforts is based on one simple thing: I am wired as an artist. I cannot help it. I am not wired to be a marketing director, or a doctor, or a political adviser, or a restaurateur—though I have worked in all of those fields and would have been "good," in the eyes of our culture, at all of those jobs.

But what I've uncovered about myself is I don't work well with my sole focus on repetitive technical or office tasks, performed year after year. I've learned to be disciplined, and though I'm social and like people, I do my best working on my own, or in a teaching environment, on creative, project-oriented work with a defined beginning, middle, and end. I have a flair for putting together words, for abstract painting, for gourmet cooking, for singing and songwriting, and for a bunch of other artistic things.

What that has meant for me is that a day-job-alone life will not work. My artistry has to be a part of my life or I get angry, irritated, and begin disliking the world and myself.

It took me years to understand that I cannot fit the round-headedness of my being into a square lifestyle. The more I pushed my artist self away for the get-ahead, status quo life, the unhappier I got. The larger pull—all the time—has been my artistry. It's always what I come back to, always what calls. That doesn't mean I have consistently shown up for it. I have blotted out parts or whole pieces of it for as many years as I have dedicated myself to it.

It took a long time for me to admit—out loud to myself, and then to the world—that I am an artist. Even now, after realizing that I am miserable when I don't do my art, that's still not the primary reason why I engage in it. Being miserable without it will propel me to get to work, but it's not the underlying reason for doing it.

The reason I do my art is because *it's worth doing*. I can go on and on about how creative work is a high calling, embellishing lavish poetics about its value, but the truth is simpler than that. It's worth doing because I am answering what my heart is calling me to do. I am answering with *action*: hearty, committed, explorative, brave, open-minded, outrageous action.

And there is nothing more powerful in the world for us artists than being that courageous.

Separate Yourself from the Hobbyist.

First off, there is nothing wrong with having artistic hobbies. Many people do and derive great joy from them. But what we're up to is to learn how to be an artist: one who uses his or her ambition to bring work out into the world in a professional way.

Why do we care if it's professional? Why not just remain an amateur? Because bringing our work out into the light of the world—even the art-dismissive culture we live in—teaches us how to reach people. It helps us see what art is about—that is, lifting the human spirit. That's what we're after: to reflect back to our fellow-humans a vision of who we are, what we see, where we are in time, and what that experience looks like and feels like.

There's something else that happens when we approach our work professionally: It makes us view our art with a critical eye. And that's important if we want to grow. It's our progress—our growth—that challenges us to perfect our voice, and to contribute something meaningful to our culture over time.

Think about how Rothko or Monet or Cezanne began. Because they brought their work out into the public eye over and over—rejecting old forms and insisting on new ones as they bucked the entrenched, artistic mores—they pressed *us* to find new ways of seeing, too. Without their insistence on professionalism, we would not have the exquisite, soul-lifting experiences of impressionism or the incredible emotion of the abstract color field.

Art is a language all its own, and we don't get as practiced at it if our work lives in secret and never sees the light of day. We're seeking some kind of universal language in art, something that moves us and others.

So, though you may be just beginning to listen to your own voice and just starting to take steps to express it, work now with an ethic of readying yourself to bring your art into the world in a professional way at a date up ahead.

Keep What You're Working on Close to Your Vest.

We don't want to tell others what we're working on artistically for one simple reason: Other people's opinions will almost always muddy the waters.

We've each had the experience of sharing something that's really important to us with someone who we think will be impressed by what we've come up with, only to have them blow us off or unintentionally demean our work.

There's nothing more demoralizing than telling an acquaintance that I'm working my ass off in my studio on a new series of abstract faces, only to then have him say, "Oh, I painted in high school and dabble a bit, too . . ." as if my professional efforts are equal to his dabbling, and then, by extension, not very important.

An experienced photographer friend of mine made a great

point about the watering-down of artistic accomplishment in her field. Since the invention of the smartphone camera, her art arena has been flooded with amateur photographers, and the value of composition and expertise has been diluted. People now tell her, "Oh, I'm a photographer, too, on my iPhone . . ." as if her years of professional work are now obsolete.

And we'll always have to field that kind of stuff when we bring our art into the world. But we can help ourselves by knowing who we're talking to, and by *saying less*—especially while we're in the beginning stages of a new and budding project or style.

As artists our confidence is like a frail sail, finely woven and just delicate enough to catch and hold the wind, so we can't afford to let other people slice it up. We need to nurture our ideas inside ourselves first, guarding our heart and our artistic vision.

If we've had some success with a particular form or style it can be tempting to keep doing the same thing over and over, and to stop exploring. And creating for the masses can work for a while, but it won't last indefinitely. It's another form of looking outside ourselves for people's approval, and it tends to bottom out after a handful of years.

Eventually, we'll need to start discovering again, to invent new ways of speaking to our audiences, and to keep listening for what's next. It's the nature of the beast. Art is commentary, a vision of some aspect of life reflected back to our heart, and it needs to keep reinventing itself to keep speaking to us.

Here's my best advice on dealing with other people's opinions and inquiries: Stop justifying. Keep what you're doing close to your vest until it's finished. Don't brag about what you're working on and don't share the details. If people you love and trust ask how your work is going, simply say, "It's going well, and I'm keeping the details to myself for the time being. Thanks for asking." And then change the subject.

Do your work in the presence of your own inspiration, your own calling, and your own heart, and don't look up until it's done.

No One Gets to Judge You.

A dear friend of mine, a professional playwright, called me once, down in the dumps because her mother had angrily accused her of selfishness for doing her art. "You only live for yourself," her mother said. "You and your selfish theater life."

Firstly, my friend is kind, loving, humble, gracious, and a delight to be with. She is not anywhere near the bell-curve-end extreme of "selfishness." And obviously, her mother was having a bad day, and that unkindness probably had more to do with her own issues than anything that had passed between them.

But something in the accusation stuck sharply in my friend's heart. And while we talked it out, I began sharing what I knew to be the spiritual truth of writing and direct-ing and acting in plays. It's a job that asks her to show audiences the intimacies of relationships—love, heartbreak, death, grief, loss, jubilation, overcoming obstacles, and many times, the character's need to pursue and overcome something with determination. In other words, I was able to share that what she does is a high calling—that she is of great service to the hundreds and thousands of people who see her work, and that she asks of others to reflect on their own behavior, to learn from mistakes and failings, and to be more loving.

We all have to have a vision for our work that's more than what it is at face value. Otherwise, the judgments of others can come crashing down on our heads and can cripple our ability to work. The simplest and easiest thought I use to stay in alignment with my art when it is challenged is this: *What is the spiritual truth of what I do?*

Painting? It's beauty, vibrancy, lushness, and emotional upliftment. Songwriting? It's the poetry of my soul, the folksy delicacy of love, heartbreak, healing, and wonder. Writing? It's the voice I speak with, a conversation about what it is to be alive as an artist, a woman, a wife, a lover, and a dweller in this gorgeous and complex world.

Who can say why we're drawn to compose symphonies and play the cello? Who gets to judge why it's important and pressing to our soul to stand up on stage and sing in a musical? Who can comb the inner realm of our will that *needs* to construct brilliantly colored abstract metal sculptures or film documentaries in developing countries?

The point is this: No one gets to judge us and we need not let them. We can set boundaries and develop the strength to get off the phone, leave the room, or generally head judg-mental comments off at the pass. And when they do land on our head, we can back off, back up, and remember that what we do is not subject to the opinions of others. We are here to create as our heart sees fit: to do good with our art, to see and invent and create and reflect back, and to enjoy doing so. It's a huge gift we offer as artists, and we get to *own* being coura-geous enough to do what we do.

There is only one right judge of how we're living as an artist and that's our own divinely given heart.

Acquire Wisdom.

Once, when I was in some emotional trouble, I worked with a terrific hypnotherapist who helped me see something pro-found about my life experience through a story he called "The Great Sword."

It seems there was a band of Japanese warriors who forged huge swords, and then burned them in the fire 1,000 times. The burning created incredible carbon designs on the metal—beautiful lines of exquisite artistry that were unique to each weapon and could not be created in any other way. The swords that made it through the 1,000 firings were given one last test. They were put into a stream, butt down and blade up, while the warriors watched. As a leaf glided down atop the water, the "Good Sword" easily sliced it in half as it floated. But when the "Great Sword" was propped into the stream, the leaf sensed its amazingly solid strength and power, and floated *around the sword.*

What we're up to as artists is about more than just producing terrific art. We are setting a path for ourselves to be the Great Sword: to be strong, determined, and a force for artistic good.

By the very nature of our work we are asking ourselves to comment on life as we know it, to practice a deeper form of honesty than is required in everyday life, and to mirror back to our fellow humans a vision of the ethereal substance and truths of our living experience. We're asking those around us to look more closely and more deeply at life and humanity, with a reverence not usually practiced. That means we have to acquire wisdom.

Everything we've ever experienced, both good and bad, becomes grist for the art mill. All of our painful failings and hurts, our joyous elation, every humorous moment we've ever stumbled upon, and each reverent witnessing of nature, flesh, and the universe goes into the heart and comes out in the form of art.

That means we cannot stay stuck in the childishness of who hurt whom and "Why me?" We need to learn to forgive. We need to learn to draw a line in the sand between ourselves and difficult people. We need to be the "Great Sword" and let drama float around us. We have to know when to take the high road so that our art and our artist's life will be protected long term, for our whole lifetime. We have to view our life not through the lens of the quick-fix, envy-laden celebrity passed off to us as "success," but through the kaleidoscope of observation, understanding, and insight.

When we understand that the path of the artist is a path of service, everything we've ever experienced will become a beautiful garden from which we can draw anything we like, and it will feed our creativity for the whole of a wise and fulfilling life.

Be a Moral Force for Your Art.

Morality, in this context, is not about doctrine-governed rules or tenets. It's about how we behave with our art; who we are; what our life testifies to. In other words, we want to do our work and bring it out into the world with right action and integrity.

And I'll go even further than that: We want to behave in a way that does not bring reproach upon our work.

Success is usually the thing that chips away at our ethics, and not just success in the big-screen, I-made-$6-million-on-my-last-project way, either. What I'm talking about is success as *attention*—that is, getting attention for our work, or for being artists in the first place.

An actor friend of mine once helped me understand this by telling me a simple story. She said, "When I finally get onto a film set—after all of the auditioning, negotiating, and the hoops I have to jump through—I get so excited I could get aroused by the doorknob. That's when I really have to watch it." Her point is this: If she doesn't keep her ethics in check, she'll be tempted to make a mess of things by using her excitement to create drama and intrigue with other cast members on the set.

And we don't want to do that. Intrigue and acting out are ways of creating distractions from our art. And self-imposed distractions are just another form of procrastination. They are self-invented ways to crash the car and send the wheels rolling down the hill with no hope of recovering them.

Sure, doing our artwork often makes us feel free and thrilled and sometimes even wild, but if we gunk up the works with bad behavior, our carefully built creative castles will crumble.

What this means in practical terms is, we don't use our acting class or our on-the-road stage production to cheat on our spouse or work the room for short-term sexual partners. We don't screw suppliers out of the money they're due for our art supplies. We pay our studio rent on time. In essence, we don't lie, cheat, or steal around our art.

Once more, our art projects are like our kids: We need to be good parents to them for our children to thrive. We want to set a good example and live inside our very frail humanity with as much honesty and ethical judgment as we can.

That doesn't mean we won't make mistakes. We will unintentionally screw up time after time, topple our ship, and have to make amends to right it. That's the nature of life-on-earth-school. But we don't use our art to *purposely* make bad choices.

Being an artist is about being truthful; not only being truthful to our creative spirit, but being an honest and clear force for action in the world. So, we take the moral high road always.

Practice Practical Inspiration.

Practical inspiration is exactly what it sounds like. It means living an inspired life, but with our feet firmly planted on planet Earth. It means living in the real world, in which we have obligations, duties, challenges, and have to show up to support ourselves, while still connecting ourselves to the divine spark of our own artistry.

It means we suit up, time and time again, stepping from the realm of the ethereal—from our calling, our intuition, and the dazzling interior vision of art forms that want to birth themselves out from inside us—and become willing to labor over them until they stand on their own two feet in the physical world.

It means holding two worlds in our heart and working with both: the invisible, grace-filled, intuitive realm and the solid ground of material, physical expression.

Our day jobs live in that land of grounded expression. And though we don't usually think of having a day job as an "inspired" experience, it actually is. It is the support that directs us to manifest things in the world—to build, to sew, to hammer, to layer, to carve, to offer, and to craft—fashioning not only art forms, but an artist's life.

Being an artist and having a day job is not our burden; it is our gift. It teaches us to be good at more than one thing. It teaches us to manage our time well, a skill that will serve us rather triumphantly when we don't need a day job anymore. It teaches us that we cannot engage in suffering or starving if we want to produce art—that we must put supports under our feet if we want to be stable enough to offer our hearts to creativity.

It shows us that we need to develop work ethics— particularly if we are multitalented and have something to say in more than one art form. Our grounded-on-earth inspiration tools teach us that we have to have practical ways of motivating ourselves—even on those days when it all goes to hell and we're laid flat out by life's crazy interruptions.

And, all of it—our day job, our life challenges, our time-pressures, and our commitment to showing up for our art anyway—reveals to us the most important thing we will ever learn on the artist's path: To put supports under our feet while we do what we love most is our blessing and our gift to our-selves, an inspired means by which we will get our artwork out into the light of day. *That's* practical inspiration.

And using it to do our artwork will fill our heart with gratitude for our own courage, our own insistent bravery, and for the audacity of our own spirit.

Learn to Measure Wealth by the Freedom You Have to Do What You Love.

There are two principles that have stood me well in my years of being an artist. They are: *Learn to measure wealth by the amount of freedom you have to do what you love to do.* And, *Learn to measure happiness by how much of your artistic heart you can give.*

Make no mistake: "The freedom we have to do what we love" is something we have to build, and work on, and insist upon, and stand up for. It is tied at the umbilical cord to the time, money, and effort we are willing to set aside for our art. It's wired into our willingness to get, and keep, a day job we can live with; one that puts long-term supports under our feet.

It has to *matter* to us to make all of the sacrifices we must make for our art. Art has to serve us in our deepest, most intimate places to make all of the effort worth it.

Wealth, as an artist, has a different meaning than our culture's literal definition. Wealth brings with it time: time to discover, to explore, to create, and to build. The wealth of our ideas, visions, and ways of seeing becomes an entire language, reflecting our life paths, culture, forms, flesh, and spirit. We encompass everything with it: the light and the dark, the uplifting and the base, the gorgeous and the bleak.

When we begin to experience wealth as the freedom to express ourselves fully in an artistic way, we will be well on the way to a happy life. When happiness is a visceral sense of having listened to and acted upon our own heart's callings, we will be rich with our own self-approval and love. When we see ourselves as a part of an intricate fabric of artistic poetry—a mirror of humanity's experience and a call to others to notice, see, pause, and reflect—we will always have a place of value in the world.

The humility it takes to lay ourselves on the tracks of our creativity is life-altering. When we feel wealthy because we're artists, we're able to trust the creative process and where it leads. We can hear it without fear.

There's an adage first proposed by Swedish psychologists, and made popular by Malcolm Gladwell that goes something like, "Mastery comes after we have 10,000 hours in some craft or art." What that idea is speaking to is the idea that we need *time in*. Consistent, brave, exploratory, long-term, boundary-breaking, courageous time in. And, as it turns out, we don't need as many as 10,000 hours to find the riches of being an artist. All we need is a regular habit of showing up for ourselves.

Remember that the word of the cultural day was that Monet couldn't paint. But he kept showing up for all of that beauty anyway. He had to find the wealth inside himself and value it, to keep going and live the life he wanted to live.

That's what we're after: to live with the gift of art as our guiding star, and to stay connected to its value, its worth, and to the exquisite, grace-filled treasure it brings into our lives.

Make a Heaven on Earth.

Artists are in a constant state of worship. We observe the world, nature, the flesh, and the spirit, and capture those essences in our work. We bring reverence to each: an experiential moment in time on canvas, on paper, in stone, in music, on a mural. We are essentially praising life.

Praise—the exquisite moment when we realize how amazing it is to just be alive—is in the soul of every work of art we do. We are worshipping life, not to bow down to it, but to walk with it, to see it with eyes wide open for all that it is. It is our unique grace as artists to be able to do that—to live life while crafting a voice from inside it, to give other human beings pause enough to remember how sweet and hard and wondrous and exquisite this tapestry of love, pain, and growth is.

It is reverence that has us blast the giant canvas with colors that flare in our heart; amazing grace that calls us to craft the human form in bronze; boundless, earthly passion that has us set the vision of a crowded city into a 50-foot collage. We are deifying what we see by making art.

We find for ourselves what Rumi wrote so many centuries ago:

The garden of the world has no limits . . .
Its presence is more beautiful than the stars

With more clarity
Than the polished mirror of your heart.

And, adding to that, Wayne Dyer's quotation:

Heaven on earth is a choice you must make, not a place you must find.

Art makes us see heaven in this world—the underpinnings of all that lies beneath every human and universal thing, the threads of the exquisite fabric of our living tapestry.

So, go on. Make a heaven on earth. Do your art.

Begin, and give yourself tools. Support yourself and live within your means. Nurture your own ideas, apart from other people's opinions. Explore. Give yourself the gift of time. Be ethical. Be courageous. Be an artistic force for good—a mirror for all of humanity. Tell the truth. Be of service to your art and to whomever it touches. Bring your work into the world with humility, professionalism, and the willingness to learn. Cultivate wisdom. Find happiness in your creative soul.

Heaven is now. You know what you have to do. Now get to work.

INDEX

accountability, 105–7, 127–29
See also showing up
amateur artists, dealing with,
177–79
annual expenses, 47, 48
apps, using, 63–64
art income, 73–74
artistry, 7–20
acting on a vision, 10–12,
16–17, 82–84
answering the call, 12–13,
79–82, 174–75
challenges of, 9–10, 15–16
healthy life skills for, 17–18
lifetime commitment of,
93–94
listening to the heart, 13–15
nurturing and supporting,
19–20
art life maps. *See* Time Maps

balance in life, 117–18, 126, 137–
38, 156
"beating the room," 88, 103–5
bill expenses, 46, 47, 50, 54–57,
64
Bill-Paying Plan, 54–57
boundaries, setting, 155–59

cash income, 42, 45
See also spending plans
circling behavior, 104–5
clarity, achieving
money, 41–43, 52–54, 67–68,
70–71, 73
time, 138–41
commitment to art, 93–94
cost of living. *See* living
expenses
creative process, 172–74, 183,
188
credit card debt, 44–46, 59, 67
criticism and pessimism, 129–33

daily needs expenses
keeping track of, 57–65
listing, 46–49
paying for, 55–57
day jobs, 21–37
appreciating, 32–33
choosing, 24–26
excelling at, 30–32
flexible jobs, 52
"good people" jobs, 26–28
leaving, 71–75
lessons from, 185–86
need for, 23–24

day jobs (*continued*)
  "secondary arts" jobs, 29–30
  setting boundaries, 155–59
  steady progress and, 35–37
  taking action, 33–35
  work ethics and, 186
debit *vs.* credit cards, 59
debt avoidance, 44–46, 59,
  67–68
Debt-Free Spending Plan, The
  (Nagler), 51, 54–55
detachment, practicing, 111–12
discipline, developing, 127–29
discovery process, 131–32
dissatisfaction in life, 169–70,
  174–75
distractions, dealing with, 133–36,
  149–50, 162–63
Divine guidance, 108–9
downsizing, 41–42, 50–52, 69–70,
  73
Dyer, Wayne, 190

ethical behavior, 183–85
  See also work ethics
expenses. *See* living expenses

finances, managing. *See* money
  management

goals. *See* time goals

happiness and wealth, 187–88
heaven on earth, 189–90

income. *See* art income; cash
  income; day jobs
inspiration, 97–98, 185–86
interest lists, 25–26, 35
invention and creativity, 172–74

jobs. *See* day jobs
judgment from others, 179–81

living expenses
  annual, 47, 48
  bills, 46, 47, 54–57, 59, 64
  cutting expenses, 49–52, 69–71,
    72–73
  daily needs, 46–49, 55–57, 57–65
  spending plans for (*see* spending
    plans)

Magic Notebook, 57–61, 64
managing money. *See* money
  management
mapping exercise. *See* Time Maps
marketing practices, 113–14
Meditation, The Walking, 99
meditation/prayer, 135
money management, 39–75
  cash funds for projects, 66–68,
    69–71
  creative funding, 51–52
  cutting expenses, 49–52, 69–71,
    72–73
  daily needs, tracking, 46–49,
    55–65
  day jobs and, 52, 71–75
  debt avoidance, 44–46, 59,
    67–68
  living on less, 69–71
  money clarity, 41–43, 52–54,
    67–68, 70–71, 73
  monthly expenses (*see* spending
    plans)
monthly spending plans. *See*
  spending plans
motivation, 167–90
  acquiring wisdom, 181–83
  answering the call, 174–75

artists as professionals, 176–77
cultivating a good attitude, 170–72
day job lessons, 185–86
dissatisfaction and, 169–70, 175
honesty and integrity, 183–85
invention and creativity, 172–74
judgment from others, 179–81
learning to say less, 177–79
praising life, 189–90
wealth and happiness, 187–88

negative thinking, 83

obligations and duties, 123, 125–26
optimism, 131
outcomes, letting go of, 110–12
"overalls," mapping, 138–41

pessimism and criticism, 129–33
privilege myth, 83–85
procrastination, 104–5, 127–28, 169–70
professionals, artists as, 176–77

Rumi, 189–90

savings needs, 47, 48, 74
scheduling time, 88–92, 99–100, 102–3
    See also time management; Time Maps
showing up, 92–93, 97–98, 107–9, 188
spending plans
    art income and, 72–75
    bill-paying and, 54–57

cash funding with, 66–68
choosing to downsize, 69–71
creating, 46–49, 51
simplicity of, 43–44
technology tools and, 62–65
value of, 65–66
spiritual truths, 179–81
Structure of Scientific Revolution, The (Kuhn), 173
support, artistic, 159–62

technology tools, 62–64
"tells," awareness of, 133–36
time goals, 105–7, 135–36, 150, 152
time guidelines, 162–65
time management, 77–94
    accountability and, 105–7, 127–29
    acting on a vision, 82–84
    answering the call, 79–82
    as lifetime commitment, 93–94
    principles of, 90–91
    prioritizing, 86–87
    privilege myth, 83–85
    scheduling time, 88–92, 99–100, 102–3
    showing up, 92–93, 97–98
    strategizing, 87–88
    wasting time, 103–5
Time Maps, 119–65
    adjusting the map, 153–55
    artistic support, 159–62
    chapter overview, 162–65
    creating, 125–26
    detailed example of, 142–48
    drawing the map, 121–22
    enjoyment, allowing for, 136–38

Time Maps (*continued*)
  fixed and flex times, 138–41
  implementing in the real world,
    148–51
  personal accountability and,
    127–29
  pessimism and, 129–33
  setting boundaries, 155–59
  variable schedules and,
    151–53
  work distractions, 133–36
timers for scheduling, 105–7, 135,
  150

Walking Meditation, The, 99
War of Art, The (Pressfield), 170
wealth and happiness, 187–88

work discipline, developing,
  127–29
work ethics, 95–118
  accountability, 105–7
  day jobs and, 186
  emotional support, 114–17
  inspiration and, 97–98
  letting go of outcomes,
    110–12
  life balance, maintaining,
    117–18, 126, 137–38, 156
  moving on, 112–14
  multiple interests, 102–3
  practicing detachment, 111–12
  showing up, 107–9
  tools for developing, 98–101
  wasting time, 103–5